C000314456

Independent Thinking on Teac[...] potential to be a game-chan[...] shows how, through self-reflect[...] ation, educators can transforn[...] and achieve better outcomes – and, more importantly, the book also recognises how pupils can help them to do just that. I shudder to think how many children might achieve more if the half a million teachers in the UK put into practice the common sense and practical advice it contains.

DAVID REESON, INDEPENDENT CONSULTANT IN SOCIAL CARE AND FORMER DIRECTOR OF KPMG

Jackie has produced a book that looks at the job of teaching from numerous angles. Written with a sense of the reality of life in classrooms, it pulls together a range of theoretical perspectives and is full of suggestions for developing the craft of teaching to improve learning for all pupils.

We all want to be better teachers, and reading *Independent Thinking on Teaching and Learning* will help us improve our practice.

MICK WATERS, PROFESSOR OF EDUCATION, UNIVERSITY OF ·WOLVERHAMPTON

Independent Thinking on Teaching and Learning is a very reflective piece of work that has a mixture of practical solutions and research-informed ideas. It is a fantastic tool for every teacher and school leader, and an excellent resource for CPD with staff. A must-read.

ELIZA HOLLIS, EXECUTIVE HEAD TEACHER, THE FOREST CE FEDERATION OF SCHOOLS

With *Independent Thinking on Teaching and Learning*, Jackie Beere offers a timeless guide which reflects on the elements of great teaching and learning through the lens of her extensive experience in the profession. Jackie considers the latest agendas and policies alongside previous versions, offering well-informed critiques of the best approaches to teaching and learning. The book is essential reading for entrants to initial teacher training, providing an up-to-date compendium of approaches, ideas, dos and don'ts that will serve them well on their journey in teaching.

LUCY WESTLEY, SENIOR LECTURER IN INITIAL TEACHER TRAINING, UNIVERSITY OF NORTHAMPTON

Independent Thinking on Teaching and Learning is perfectly timed as we enter an era of accessible and plentiful research on metacognition, cognitive science and pedagogy.

As time-poor professionals, it's helpful to have clear navigation to bridge the gap between research and practice, while not forgetting the emotional aspect of teaching. In Jackie's own words: 'I have sifted through the jargon and pulled out what I believe to be the very best practice that works to help our children learn.' And this is exactly what you will find in this book. It is an incisive and comprehensive guide that draws on trustworthy research and presents it in a digestible form, supported by reasoning from classroom experience. It has lots of practical ideas to help busy teachers in any stage of their career, with each chapter being relevant for the challenges faced in modern-day teaching.

Overall, this book is a superb addition to any teaching and learning library – and is a resource that will surely stand the test of time.

GAVIN BOYLE, DIRECTOR OF LEARNING, ST CHRISTOPHER'S SCHOOL

TEACHING AND LEARNING

Jackie Beere

DEVELOPING INDEPENDENCE AND RESILIENCE
IN ALL TEACHERS AND LEARNERS

ındependent
thinking press

First published by

Independent Thinking Press
Crown Buildings, Bancyfelin, Carmarthen, Wales, SA33 5ND, UK
www.independentthinkingpress.com

and

Independent Thinking Press
PO Box 2223, Williston, VT 05495, USA
www.crownhousepublishing.com

Independent Thinking Press is an imprint of Crown House Publishing Ltd.

Edited by Ian Gilbert.

The Independent Thinking On ... series is typeset in Azote, Buckwheat TC Sans, Cormorant Garamond and Montserrat.

The Independent Thinking On ... series cover style was designed by Tania Willis www.taniawillis.com.

British Library Cataloguing-in-Publication Data
A catalogue entry for this book is available from the British Library.

Print ISBN 978-178135339-4
Mobi ISBN 978-178135350-9
ePub ISBN 978-178135351-6
ePDF ISBN 978-178135352-3

LCCN 2019953748

Printed and bound in the UK by
Gomer Press, Llandysul, Ceredigion

This book is dedicated to my wonderful mum and my amazing grandchildren, Lyla, Josh and Taran, who all represent my fortunate past and my precious hopes for the future.

When writing this book, I was always thinking about all the inspiring teachers I have known and how much our future, as a nation, depends on them.

FOREWORD BY IAN GILBERT

Since establishing Independent Thinking in 1994, we have worked hard to share with educators around the world our belief that there is always another way. The Independent Thinking On ... series of books is an extension of that work, giving a space for great educators to use their words and share great practice across a number of critical and relevant areas of education.

Independent Thinking on Teaching and Learning takes us right back to where it all really started, when I was fresh-faced and fresh out of teacher training, and no one had heard of academies, Ofsted or, indeed, me. I had come into the world of education (as a teacher of French) to be able to work directly with young people on learning and motivation, and I knew that there were many different approaches that could be used in the classroom to make things better for all young people.

While we didn't have Twitter as a vehicle for people to tell me how stupid I was to suggest that students might learn in different ways, it meant that we could have real conversations about the nature of teaching and learning and about how, although learning is learning, we don't have to treat everyone the same in the classroom.

And who knows, maybe some of the things people talked about back then didn't do all that they claimed to do, but they did something and that something was worthwhile. According to Durham University researcher Steve Higgins, although the claims made about 'pseudo-scientific' practices were wrong, 'the practices undertaken in schools may have some education value for other reasons'. Indeed, he suggests that those claiming such approaches can't work because the science behind them is flawed are themselves displaying a 'lack of critical (or scientific) thinking as brain-gym and NLP might be reliably effective at achieving certain outcomes, just not for the reasons the proponents expound'.[1]

In other words, teachers aren't stupid and who is anyone to tell them that what works doesn't work? After all, as we have been saying for a long time now, there is always another way, especially in the world of education. Which is why long-time Independent Thinking Associate Jackie Beere is still so much in demand for sharing her insightful, compassionate and rigorous approaches to teaching and learning across the UK and further afield.

And why this book is such a perfect addition to a series for teachers which is all about thinking for yourself.

IAN GILBERT
BIRMINGHAM

---

1 S. Higgins, A Recent History on Teaching Thinking. In R. Wegerif, L. Li and J. Kaufman (eds), *The Routledge International Handbook of Research on Teaching Thinking* (Abingdon and New York: Routledge, 2015), pp. 19-28 at p. 21.

ACKNOWLEDGEMENTS

I would like to thank Ian Gilbert for persuading me to write this book and renew my passion for the most important profession in the world. We have shared our journey through decades of change in education initiatives and in life – and if I ever want a new perspective, I know who to turn to. He has gathered around him an amazing group of educationalists at Independent Thinking, who never fail to have the energy and passion required to inspire. I want to thank the Independent Thinking family for giving me decades of opportunities to keep finding 'another way'.

Everyone at Crown House has always been so supportive, patient and helpful throughout the long and challenging process of writing – I couldn't imagine working with a nicer bunch of people.

Without my husband, John, to provide me with encouragement and feedback, this book would not have seen daylight, so a massive thank you to him and also to my daughters, who continue to inspire me. Since the arrival of my grandchildren, my belief in the teaching profession and the power it has to influence the next generation has multiplied. I want to thank all the teachers who work so hard to mould our children into great learners despite the challenges of the 21st century. We need to value and reward them for the vital work they do.

CONTENTS

FIRST THOUGHTS

Teachers are so important. According to Ron Berger, the best question you can ask any pupil or member of staff to find out what a school is like is: what does it take 'to fit in, socially and academically' around here?[1]

And now, at last, Ofsted agrees: 'Inspectors must use all their evidence to evaluate what it is like to attend the school.'[2]

Make no mistake, it is the teachers that create the experience of school for the pupils.

The advice in this book draws on the latest educational research and many of the Ofsted descriptors of 'outstanding teaching' that have been produced over the years. Even if they are not the latest guidance, they are still useful references for what success looks like. However, this book is determined not to merely link practice to Ofsted's latest sound bites, because they change with every government or secretary of state for education. Each has a different agenda and tends to dispose of previous policy for political reasons. Remember initiatives like Every Child Matters, SEAL (social and emotional aspects of learning), PLTs (personal, learning and thinking skills), character education, personal development, curriculum intent, AfL (assessment for learning), safeguarding and citizenship? All have had their time in the sun and some, as you will see in this book, are still relevant and useful.

---

1   R. Berger, *An Ethic of Excellence: Building a Culture of Craftsmanship with Students* (Portsmouth, NH: Heinemann, 2003), p. 35.

2   Ofsted, *School Inspection Handbook*. Ref: 190017 (2019), p. 39. Available at: https://www.gov.uk/government/publications/school-inspection-handbook-eif.

This book aims to be a timeless guide to great teaching and learning, aimed at new teachers and teachers who want to renew their passion. I have sifted through the jargon and pulled out what I believe to be the very best practice that works to help our children learn. You have the assurance that the advice in this book is not included simply to satisfy this administration or current inspection framework; it is included because it has been tried and tested by great teachers over decades.

The current focus on 'evidence-led' practice is helpful, but every child is an individual. We always need to remember that while research can claim that a technique works brilliantly, in practice we might find that it doesn't work for certain children. Research can also be contradictory. Is red wine healthy or dangerous, and what really is the best way to learn to read and write? This book is based on my own judgement, informed by evidence, but grounded in my experience of the huge variety of human responses to learning in different contexts. Use this book to find out what works, then find out what works for you and your individual pupils and build on that to fulfil their potential.

There has never been a more important time to be a teacher. Our young people seem more fragile and insecure than ever. This insecurity can destroy any chance of happiness and blight potential achievement. Social media dominates their lives and has the capacity to create a contagious culture of comparison and, thereby, self-judgement. Everything from their looks, the music they choose to listen to and the places they go can be measured by 'likes' and 'friends'. Teachers can offer an antidote to this pressure by modelling and nurturing the love and support for each other that is innate in all of us. Helping children to be resilient as they learn and giving them thinking strategies – metacognitive tools

– will protect them from taking social media – or themselves – too seriously.

Teacher recruitment and retention is a serious problem, especially for schools in disadvantaged areas that need great teachers the most. Our school leaders are facing massive challenges – coping with budget cuts and ever-changing political diktats – but they know that their main priority is growing wonderful teachers. Teachers are all individuals with their own unique strengths and challenges: there has never been only one way to be a great teacher. I hope that teachers and leaders can use this book to build on their strengths and challenge their weaknesses so that they make the greatest impact on each and every child's academic and personal progress.

Every child in this country will become a more resilient, productive, confident and generous citizen if they learn with teachers who care enough to show them that they have limitless potential to be happy and successful.

> *Everything can be taken from a man but one thing: the last of the human freedoms – to choose one's attitude in any given set of circumstances, to choose one's own way.*
>
> **VICTOR FRANKL**[3]

---

3   V. Frankl, *Man's Search for Meaning* (New York: Pocket Books, 1984 [1959]), p. 86.

CHAPTER 1

UNLEASHING YOUR TEACHER POWER

Have you any idea how powerful you are? If you have any doubt about the difference you make to the lives of the children in your class, consider your own education. Can you think of the teacher who inspired you or the teacher who belittled you with a comment that still resonates in your adult life?

No child remembers a secretary of state for education or Ofsted chief inspector, but every child remembers a teacher or teaching assistant (TA) who believed in them or shared a passion that became contagious. It's often not the stuff they taught us that we remember, but the way they connected with us. The way they really listened, cared about us and understood our world. The way they modelled their own passion and beliefs, so we could tune in and enjoy the thrill of learning.

As teachers, we may have experienced a moment of flow when a class is truly engaged and entranced by our message. It's a delight to connect with our learners in this way – but it takes much more than a good lesson plan and an interesting topic to do it. What makes it happen is often that unspoken humility and love in our body language, facial expression and eye contact that seeks a human connection first – and educates later.

WHAT DO THE LEARNERS SAY?

Pupils at two excellent schools made the following anecdotal comments when asked about their school experiences:

	Learners from Years 4–6	Learners from Years 7–11
What's your favourite thing about your school?	How nice people are to each other. All the trips we go on. The library, because it has a lovely range of books. Everything we learn is interesting and fun.	Seeing my friends. Teachers who are really helpful. People with individual needs get help. Trips.
What stops you learning?	Personal worries and concerns. Sitting with friends who want to chat about stuff and distract me. When other children chat and don't get on with the work.	Bad behaviour. When teachers go over the top with their power. Weak teachers.
What sort of teaching and learning helps you make the most progress?	Working with lots of different people helps me. When the teacher is enthusiastic and makes the lesson	Seeing it being done. Knowing why – the reasons help me remember.

	Learners from Years 4–6	Learners from Years 7–11
	fun. A teacher who has a lively voice and sounds as if they enjoy teaching us really makes me want to learn. I like it when we tackle a problem together with a class goal – because we struggle together. By working with other people you can learn so much about a subject. Learning from friends works for me and seems to help my brain. We work in partners for reading and editing work and we work in groups for project work. When a teacher does the unexpected, it really helps us remember. I like it when our teacher links the lesson to something we can remember, like Neptunes for numerators and	Having the steps shown to us. Working with friends. Playing games and group work. Mini quizzes and making flashcards or mind maps for homework. Peer assessment when you can see another person's work. When teachers mark to improve our work, not nitpick. Teachers modelling answers. Acronyms and songs like the photosynthesis song.[1]

---

1 See https://www.youtube.com/watch?v=C1_uez5WX1o.

	Learners from Years 4–6	Learners from Years 7–11
	Dinosaurs for denominators in fractions. And she draws a line with her hand and calls rounding 'rainbows', which makes it easy to remember.	
	My teacher makes us repeat over and over again as a class when we learn new vocabulary – like saying 'absorb' every day so it really, really sinks in.	
	We have balloons with difficult words written on in the classroom, so it reminds us to use them in our work.	
What do you need to do to fit in around here? (A question to discover the values and culture of the school as defined by how pupils experience it.)	You have to be able to do lots of different things – help friends, play sport, do work – be flexible and be willing to go for it. Be kind to each other. Act with respect to others.	Care about exam results. Get on with teachers. Don't be completely good. Be me. Our school motto is 'exceeding expectations'.

	Learners from Years 4–6	Learners from Years 7–11
	Be yourself and you will be fine.	
	Be active, don't be a passenger and always try your best.	
	Do what the school motto says.	

So, how can you really connect with and enthuse your pupils – even the most difficult ones – and turn them on to learning?

CONNECT AND CALIBRATE

Great teachers tune in and connect with their pupils, greeting them by name with a smile and noticing their mood. During the lesson they constantly respond to the pupils' moods, calibrating their voice and body language, improvising and tuning in to keep the human connection when the education begins. Demonstrate the behaviours shown in the image that follows with love and a determination to open their minds to learning.

Teaching can be an exhausting and exhilarating profession – on the same day! It's not how you feel or what happens to you that matters; it's how you connect and calibrate that matters in the classroom. How you respond to pupils depends on how you perceive the world. This chapter will help you discover how to choose the mindset

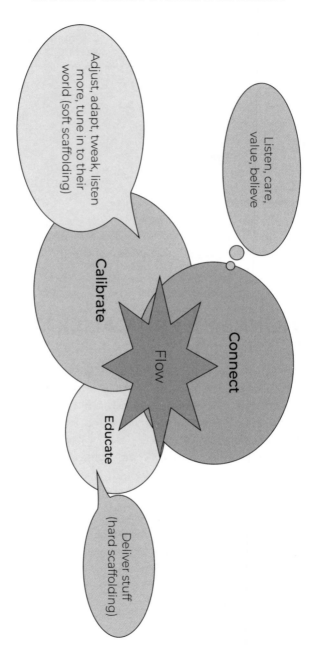

that will help you make the most of the power you have as a teacher.

You don't have to be a certain type of person to be a great teacher. Check out these examples of great teachers with whom I have worked:

Teacher A: the showstopper. He dresses up in relevant costumes and uses drama to get the content across to his pupils. He loves to think up unusual ideas or challenges and is passionate about his subject.

Teacher B: the quietly spoken grafter. Dedicated to his learners, he plans their learning meticulously to meet individual needs. He uses stories and international themes to generate interest.

Teacher C: the edgy, sassy teacher. She uses classroom technology to enhance learning experiences. Her previous life as a journalist and experience with her own children has made her determined to learn how to make a difference in education for the 21st century.

Cognitive scientist Daniel Willingham said that good teachers won't all have the same style, but the two things that they have in common – that matter most for pupils – are that they demonstrably like their pupils and that they present the learning in a way that makes it interesting. The emotional bond between pupils and teachers, for better or worse, has a big impact on learning.[2]

It's important to really know your pupils and the context of their achievement in your school. That means knowing which groups need challenging, supporting or pushing. Always be particularly concerned about how you're helping

2   D. T. Willingham, *Why Don't Students Like School? A Cognitive Scientist Answers Questions About How the Mind Works and What It Means for the Classroom* (San Francisco, CA: Jossey-Bass, 2009), p. 65.

those children who show up on your school data as not making enough progress, especially with literacy and numeracy skills. These may be the ones who struggle, coast or need more challenge.

CHOOSE YOUR MINDSET

Your mindset *is* a choice that eventually becomes an unconscious habit. How you think about your job and your pupils comes from the inside out and will define your experience as a teacher. Decide now to suspend your disbelief and take control of your thinking. It will help you become a better teacher and, as a major side benefit, it will help every other aspect of your life. It did this for me.

In John Hattie's seminal work *Visible Learning for Teachers*, he argues that the most successful teachers and school leaders believe that 'success and failure in pupil learning is about what they, as teachers or leaders, did or did not do' and that successful leaders nurture this way of thinking in their teachers. 'We are', says Hattie, 'change agents!'[3]

Hattie goes on to outline eight 'mindframes' that teachers and leaders have which maximise impact on learning, saying that they:

- Believe that their core task is to evaluate the effect of their teaching.

- Believe that success and failure in student learning is about what *they* did or did not do.

- Want to talk more about the learning than the teaching.

---

3 J. Hattie, *Visible Learning for Teachers: Maximizing Impact on Learning* (Abingdon and New York: Routledge, 2012), p. 183.

- See assessment as feedback about the impact of their teaching.

- Engage in dialogue with their pupils and *listen* to them.

- Enjoy the challenge and avoid making excuses or just 'doing their best'.

- Believe that it is their role to develop positive relationships in classrooms/staffrooms.

- Inform everyone about the language of learning.

You can't change the pupil's home background, the school's lack of funding or Ofsted's latest demands. The only thing you can *always* change is the way you see things – especially the way you think about your job: a job that changes lives.

Hattie drew some crucial conclusions about nurturing beliefs and values that impact on our thinking. Our school culture is underpinned by the principles that create mind-sets which, in turn, shape the actions and attitudes of staff and pupils.

We need to believe that we are evaluators, change agents, adaptive learning experts, seekers of feedback about our impact, and be engaged in dialogue and challenge about learning. We need to see opportunity in error, that there is no failure – only feedback – and spread the message about how powerful we can be as teachers and the impact that we have on learning. It's encouraging to realise that the most important quality needed to become a great teacher is being self-reflective about the job! This is something you can master by being determined to think purposefully in a way that works to make you the best teacher you can be.

Make no mistake: the way you think makes you the teacher you are.

So, what are the habits and behaviours of the most successful teachers? A quick survey of teachers on Twitter produced this Wordle:

Where do all these essential behaviours of the very best teachers come from? We all hold fundamental principles and beliefs, out of which come the values we believe to be important. From these emerge our mindframes or mindsets (the ways in which we unconsciously think about the world and which, in turn, affect our attitudes and actions). These attitudes and actions can then become unconscious habits and personality traits that can have a positive or negative effect on our performance.

The wise words of Andy Griffith and Mark Burns sum up how teachers model brilliant learning every day for their class:

> *Teachers must personally demonstrate the qualities and behaviours they expect from their learners by consistently living those qualities and behaviours themselves.*[4]

LOSE THOSE LIMITING BELIEFS AND FIXED MINDSETS

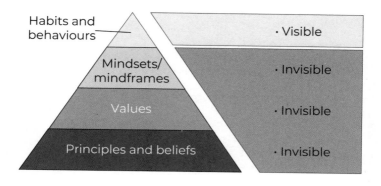

Never underestimate the power of the principles, beliefs and values that rule your life. They constantly work away in your unconscious mind, creating thoughts, inner dialogue,

---

4 A. Griffith and M. Burns, *Teaching Backwards* (Carmarthen: Crown House Publishing, 2014), p. 15.

vocabulary, behaviours, attitudes and – sometimes – fixed, inflexible mindsets that define who you are. Once mindsets are fixed, or habitual, you don't even realise that they are there – but they drive you unconsciously to make choices and decisions which mould your personality and preferences.

> *Watch your thoughts, for they become words.*
>
> *Watch your words, for they become actions.*
>
> *Watch your actions, for they become habits.*
>
> *Watch your habits, for they become character.*
>
> *Watch your character, for it becomes your destiny.*
>
> **FRANK OUTLAW**[5]

Consider the statements that follow. Are they describing you?

- I'm not really into computers.
- Meeting new people makes me nervous.
- I've never been good at maths.
- I wouldn't dance at a party – let alone for the school panto.
- I'm always late – it's in my genes!
- I would never drive in London.
- I always panic during a lesson observation.
- Eating in company makes me nervous.
- I never want to stand up and speak in public.

5   See https://quoteinvestigator.com/2013/01/10/watch-your-thoughts/.

Psychologist Carol Dweck suggested in her influential book *Mindset*, based on 20 years of research, that we all have beliefs that transform our psychology and thereby our life.[6] We can believe our qualities and intelligence are fixed in stone and part of our identity or we believe that we can change and grow through learning and experience.

Examine the beliefs that fed and grew the fixed mindset thoughts above and made them become your reality. Challenge this with questions like, 'Why am I thinking like that?', 'Is that really true?' and 'How could I change that?'

Our unconscious mind puts our own perceptual frame around everything we experience.

Do you see the good or the evil? Can you switch back and forth easily? What about that difficult boy in your class – do you see him as sparky and interesting or annoying and nasty? Can you change your mind? If you are going to an important interview, do you find yourself rehearsing a pessimistic inner dialogue like: 'Well, I probably won't get it', 'My mind will go blank', 'They won't like me'? Much of this thinking is unconscious but it influences everything. For example, it's easy for us teachers to get into the habit of blaming the kids, the parents or ourselves when something goes wrong – stereotyping certain kinds of learners and creating negative discourse in the staffroom. Habits

---

6   C. Dweck, *Mindset: The New Psychology of Success* (New York: Ballantine Books, 2006), p. 7.

start off as a choice, like aiming to arrive early, sitting in that same chair in the staffroom or choosing to moan. But once they become embedded, they become automatic (habitual). We don't even realise that this is what we do – unless we step back and reflect on and reframe our thinking. This is a healthy habit for us, and for our pupils. You *can* change your thinking, your attitudes and your beliefs!

TAKE CONTROL: USE METACOGNITION

Metacognition is simply a heightened awareness of the way we think and the way in which we see the world. I call this 'thinking on purpose'.[7] It means standing back from your thinking and looking at it. It means questioning how our thoughts work, where they come from and how we can change them or just let them go. When we use metacognition and become more conscious of our thinking, we can reframe situations and become more objective, reflective and effective. Unfortunately, we don't always question the thoughts that form our mindset.

Thinking on purpose, rather than in an unconscious, random, unmonitored way, can help you change your mindset when you need to. It gives us, and our pupils, the ability to deliberately nurture positive growth mindsets. The ability to do this can be very powerful, especially for teachers and pupils who are under pressure to perform. It's also a valuable habit for learning and can help all of us develop new approaches to learning challenges.

---

7   J. Beere, *Grow: Change Your Mindset, Change Your Life – a Practical Guide to Thinking on Purpose* (Carmarthen: Crown House Publishing, 2016).

Metacognition has been proven to be one of the most cost-effective ways to improve progress, especially for disadvantaged children. The Education Endowment Foundation, who were behind the famous Teaching and Learning Toolkit,[8] found that 'Metacognition and self-regulation approaches have consistently high levels of impact, with pupils making an average of seven months' additional progress.'[9]. Chapter 2 will explore the use of metacognition to develop those beliefs and behaviours that the best teachers share.

DON'T GENERALISE

Mo Gawdat, in his inspiring book *Solve for Happy*, offers valuable reminders about how our thinking can make us generalise, exaggerate, predict and trigger emotional reactions unnecessarily.[10] See this example of how micro-coaching during a staffroom conversation can help find the truth of a situation:

My class is a nightmare. (Exaggeration)

Have you really had a nightmare featuring them?

Well, no, but they're impossible to keep quiet. (Exaggeration)

They'll push me over the edge. (Prediction, emotion)

Is that true? Is there anything that does keep them quiet?

---

8   See https://educationendowmentfoundation.org.uk/evidence-summaries/teaching-learning-toolkit.

9   See https://educationendowmentfoundation.org.uk/evidence-summaries/teaching-learning-toolkit/meta-cognition-and-self-regulation/.

10 M. Gawdat, *Solve for Happy: Engineer Your Path to Joy* (London: Bluebird, 2017).

Occasionally, but ... they don't want to work hard. (Label)

All of them?

No, it's mainly those boys. (Label)

They don't seem to appreciate anything I do for them and it makes me feel like a rubbish teacher. (Emotion)

So the majority of the class are OK and appreciate your teaching?

Well, yes ... (The truth)

And what worked well with your class last week?

They all enjoyed the drama work on the Vikings ...

The chatter in your head is rarely the truth. It's full of NATs (negative automatic thoughts). These include predictions, labels, emotions, exaggeration and hypothesising. Micro-coaching challenges your brain's nasty tricks with the truth.

Our sympathetic response may be to agree what a nightmare the kids are, to make our colleague feel better. However, a coaching conversation is so much more helpful in creating an optimistic culture and defusing the impact our inner dialogue has on our state of mind and body. Disabusing ourselves of the belief that everything we think is necessarily true is a real advantage in pursuing contentment and clarity of thinking.

Our brains are always dual processing – working on two levels – when making decisions (see how this works in learning on page 153).[11] Our subconscious works quickly,

---

11 See https://conceptually.org/concepts/dual-processing-theory.

looking for danger (which in our evolutionary history was protective), giving us our immediate emotional gut feeling – and often resulting in negative automatic thinking. It has banked years of experiences on which to base these reactions but, when working on problems, we need to use our conscious thinking. However, our conscious mind is slower and more deliberate as it works through possibilities. Reflection time can give us an alternative to the knee-jerk response in any situation, while encouraging cognitive flexibility, curiosity and, ultimately, a more empathetic, intellectual approach to emotional challenges.

We don't always realise how much our unconscious mind is influencing us and our mindset for learning. Thinking on purpose gives us a simple way to step back from our intuitive, often negative, thinking and check that it isn't laden with unhelpful habits. For example, my own feeling that 'I always get lost when driving in big cities' often gets in the way of consciously following a simple route to my destination!

Charles Duhigg, in *The Power of Habit*, examined the neuroscience of habit and made a compelling case for acknowledging and challenging our default settings where this type of limiting thinking had become an unconscious habit:

> *Then we stopped making a choice and the behaviour became automatic. It's a natural consequence of our neurology. And by understanding how it happens, you can rebuild those patterns in whichever way you choose.*[12]

12 C. Duhigg, *The Power of Habit: Why We Do What We Do and How to Change* (London: William Heinemann, 2012), p. xvii.

DEVELOP A GROWTH MINDSET FOR YOURSELF AND YOUR LEARNERS

Carol Dweck suggests that teachers with the habits which define a growth mindset make the most difference to the progress and performance of their pupils.[13] Her research suggests that those with a growth mindset believe that change and growth are possible and desirable. They welcome challenge and relish struggle because they have a fundamental belief that they can learn from mistakes and feedback. This way of seeing the world enhances resilience because it uses feedback as information, not judgement, so avoids enhancing negative thinking habits.

You'll see in Chapter 5 how important it is for pupils to be willing to work hard at embedding knowledge into long-term memory. Daniel Willingham agrees with Dweck and considers how to help slower learners, stressing that 'intelligence can be changed through sustained hard work'.[14] Nature and nurture can define intelligence, but it is the child's attitude to learning that enables intelligence to grow through practice and engagement with challenge. He stresses, 'intelligence is malleable. It can be improved'.[15]

Of course, there are limits to our potential achievement – I will never be a great pianist, for example – but progress is always possible, if we think it is! Some say this gives slower learners false hope and fake optimism, leading ultimately to disappointment. However, my experience of pupils over several decades is that they continually surprise us. The pupil with special educational needs (SEN) who got no GCSEs but went on to run his own garden landscaping business and own a flat at 22 years old shows me how

---

13 Dweck, *Mindset.*

14 Willingham, *Why Don't Students Like School?*, p. 170.

15 Willingham, *Why Don't Students Like School?*, p. 179.

school doesn't always predict final outcomes. Maybe schools should be judged by what pupils have done ten years after they have left rather than on how they performed over a few days in summer!

What is the purpose of education? Surely it is to stimulate a lifelong love of learning and thereby prepare a child for a successful life in the 21st century? If so, then what is the value of GCSE exams that dominate the curriculum from Year 9 – exams defined by a number, testing often redundant material, giving only a snapshot of the stuff kids know – and which are then used as a damaging and unreliable measure of intelligence – and self-worth? GCSE exams are neither a reliable indicator of capability nor an inspiring intellectual springboard for teenage learners – yet they often dominate the curriculum for three or more crucial years. Is it time for a rethink?

Pupils who believe that intelligence can be improved with hard work get higher grades than those 'who believe intelligence is an immutable trait'.[16] It makes sense that teachers who have a passionate belief that they can help children become more intelligent will be the most effective at doing just that.

Data shows that teachers improve during their first five years then plateau as they gain experience because they then frequently fail to use self-critique, reflection and feedback to continually improve their practice.[17] Regular training events and annual appraisals are often not enough to ensure that teachers are engaged in the relentless endeavour to improve their teaching and put new ideas

---

16 Willingham, *Why Don't Students Like School?*, p. 180.
17 See Willingham, *Why Don't Students Like School?*, p. 192, and P. Watson, Most Teachers Reach a Performance Plateau Within a Few Years According to Research, *Montrose 42* [blog] (12 April 2013). Available at: https://montrose42. wordpress.com/2013/04/12/most-teachers-reach-a-performance-plateau-within-a-few-years-according-to-research/.

into practice to raise achievement. The best teachers consciously try to learn from one another and improve their practice and model this useful learning behaviour for their pupils.

Later, in Chapter 7, I'll explore peer coaching and how it challenges our thinking with the truth – helping us to continually improve our practice – and is an excellent way to develop resilience and a collaborative culture in the staffroom and in the classroom. The next chapter explores how you can build and rebuild your own thinking habits to become a great teacher and role model for your pupils.

My work matters – for every child, every day.

KEY POINTS

- The school life that children experience is created by their teachers.

- Teachers are powerful, especially when they believe that they are.

- You can choose to believe that you are a great teacher.

- Our experiences are created from the inside out.

- Our brains can trick us into believing unhelpful things.

- Having a growth mindset means you believe that intelligence can be grown by making the effort to learn from mistakes and feedback.

- The best teachers believe that they can make a difference and make their pupils believe it too!

When Daniel Willingham asked people, 'Who was the most important teacher in your life?' the answers were almost always related to emotional impact. For example, among the reasons given for their choices were statements like, 'She made me believe in myself.'[18]

---

18 Willingham, *Why Don't Students Like School?*, p. 186.

CHAPTER 2

TAKING CONTROL USING METACOGNITION

DEVELOP GREAT THINKING BEHAVIOURS USING METACOGNITION

The very best teachers have great beliefs and behaviours around learning and nurture those as habits in their learners. You can learn how to use metacognition to take control of your thinking habits so that you can be the teacher you want to be. As Andrew Curran found when he studied billions of dollars' worth of research about the human brain:

> [Our] unique human ability [is] to be able to turn our thoughts inwards and observe ourselves and our own mental life. This is an extraordinarily powerful observation because it is only through this ability that you can understand your own emotions and hence the emotions of others.[1]

Self-evaluating your own thinking and actions is therefore vital to becoming the best teacher you can be, because to be outstanding, teachers constantly need to think about and then adapt and tweak their practice until it works.

---

1 A. Curran, *The Little Book of Big Stuff About the Brain* (Carmarthen: Crown House Publishing, 2008), p. 22.

Improvisation when a lesson plan isn't working, by constantly connecting and calibrating, is true mastery of your vocation. Outstanding teachers embrace challenge and change, constantly modelling this for their pupils. As Carol Dweck observes:

great teachers believe in the growth of the intellect and talent, and they are fascinated with the process of learning.[2]

Dweck's decades of psychological research work create a powerful argument for the importance of approaching our goals with a growth, rather than a fixed, mindset. Stephen Covey's influential work on the habits of highly successful people has also inspired generations to consider how they can think differently to create better outcomes:

By consistently applying the principles contained in these habits, you can bring about positive changes in any relationship or situation. You can become an agent of change.[3]

There are seven behaviours that can help you to nurture your growth mindset. Remind yourself of these behaviours frequently – until they sink into your unconscious and become part of who you are. They will become the bedrock for your teaching and motivate you throughout your career:

---

2   Dweck, *Mindset*, p. 194.

3   S. R. Covey, *The 7 Habits of Highly Effective Families* (London: Simon & Schuster, 1998), p. 17.

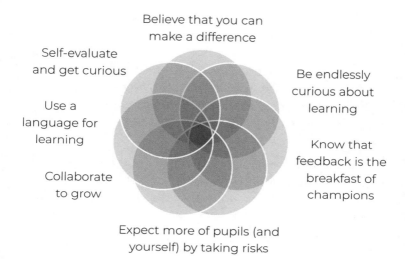

Believe that you can make a difference

Self-evaluate and get curious

Be endlessly curious about learning

Use a language for learning

Know that feedback is the breakfast of champions

Collaborate to grow

Expect more of pupils (and yourself) by taking risks

BEHAVIOUR 1: SELF-EVALUATE AND GET CURIOUS

Know yourself – know your impact: 'I know what difference I am making to my pupils and why it works or doesn't work.'

Do you have your own process of self-evaluation that helps you calibrate and adjust your teaching so that it works more effectively every day? All schools must have a self-evaluation process that enables them to reflect on their performance. You can replicate this in microcosm with your own ongoing self-evaluation process – measuring your success, learning from your mistakes, reflecting on your judgements and planning your next move on the journey towards brilliance.

Being prepared to really analyse the impact of your teaching is the secret to real success. Not just in terms of long-term outcomes – exam results and test results – but also in terms of getting wise to the effect you are having in each and every lesson – with each and every pupil – so that you can better connect and calibrate, amend and address your classroom practice. Common sense? If so, how is it done?

First, develop your awareness. Get your antennae out, detect what is and isn't working, look at body language and facial expressions, and notice the work that pupils are producing during the lesson. Ask: why did that lesson go well? How did that pupil do on that task? What feedback can I give the quiet, clever boy who never does much? How can I help that struggling learner to develop new strategies – and get her parents to help too? Watch out, however, for unconscious prejudice and labelling. The only way to check this out is to ask yourself the question: 'Is that thinking really true?' – for example, when your intuition is telling you that this child looks like trouble!

Second, seek feedback about how your teaching is affecting the progress of different learners. Listen to comments and conversations. Note what pupils say in answer to questions and in discussions. Note how they sit, how hard they work, how often they give you feedback, what their parents say, how punctual they are to your lessons, whether they attend, do your homework or ask you how you are, and how they ask you the classic question, 'What are we doing today, Miss?' Tune in to their behaviour so that you can honestly evaluate how your teaching is going. All of this is rich intelligence that will give you vital clues about your impact.

Get curious about why some lessons or strategies work and others don't. Be willing to connect and calibrate and be excited that you are still learning. Take great pleasure in finding that you have helped them really 'get it' by connecting the learning and making it memorable.

I'd no idea that changing the seating arrangement would be so challenging for them.

That's interesting – she's never worked that hard. What am I doing right today?

Exactly what *does* my class need to do next to make good progress? What extra help will Emma need, and what can I give Josh that will ensure he is fully challenged?

Learning log notes: Tuesday. Maths. Year 6.		
Plus	**Minus**	**Interesting**
Prompt start	Board game starter took too long	Work finished very quickly
Groups worked well		New feedback/ response policy is working for half the pupils
Murat made outstanding progress	Ben distracted	
	Pace led to messy presentation	
Plenary really nailed progress through success criteria	Forgot homework	Sent early finishers outside to find examples of angles – brilliant outcomes

According to Willingham, to keep improving your teaching as a cognitive skill you need to keep deepening your subject knowledge and enriching your teaching skills through practice.[4] Keep a note of plus, minus and interesting points about each lesson, week and term. This can be a rough mind map or observations in a notebook, on your phone or tablet, or in a more formal portfolio. It doesn't matter if you never read them again; the act of simply writing it down will help you evaluate, synthesise and act on your conclusions. However, your notes could eventually become a teacher's blog or book and will certainly be a very useful and amusing reference in years to come.

This mindset of self-evaluation will inevitably lead you to try action research projects, which you can share with your colleagues. These don't have to be major academic experiments in controlled conditions, but could be simple, small-scale adventures into assessing what works and what doesn't. For example:

CASE STUDY: HOW DID I GET STEPHEN TO PRODUCE MORE WRITTEN WORK?

I'd been experimenting with using music to inspire my Year 11 English bottom set and had discovered that nothing pleased everyone, so I was about to give up. However, I noticed that my most challenging pupil, Stephen, who couldn't sit still, let alone focus enough to write for 40 minutes, seemed much calmer listening to music, so I allowed him to put on his headphones and write an essay under controlled conditions for coursework.

4   Willingham, *Why Don't Students Like School?*, p. 190.

He sat and wrote quietly and industriously. I was amazed when I saw that he produced more complex sentences, better handwriting and quality analysis that was at least two grades superior to anything he had done before. I listened in on his headphones and was shocked to hear screamingly loud dance trance music – a horrible noise. But it worked for him and his essay reflected his true ability. I shared this with colleagues and used the technique again as a brain distractor with pupils with attention deficit hyperactivity disorder (ADHD) – with lots of positive anecdotal feedback about outcomes.

CASE STUDY: HOW DID JED SUDDENLY CHANGE HIS ATTITUDE TO LEARNING?

'This is boring!' Year 5 Jed had been saying this since Year 4 and spent much of his time staring out of the window, longing to be back on the farm helping his dad. He was a bright boy who was just coasting along, much more interested in football and his career goal of working in the family business. He did the minimum required to make basic progress, but he had so much more potential. I decided to run a session about the brain and how it grows when you challenge it. The class did some research on the brain and intelligence, which they loved, and we talked about growing neural pathways and strategies to develop a growth mindset – like stretching your comfort zone. We discussed emotional intelligence and optimism, taking our mood temperature and considering how it impacted on learning. It was so different to our usual projects that Jed was more engaged than usual and asked if he could take home a mood monitor to try out on his mum!

At the end of this project, Jed came to me when all his mates had gone out and asked, 'Does this mean if I don't learn stuff, 'cos sometimes I don't really try, my brain is shrinking?'

You can imagine my excitement at his insight, and I saw real progress in Jed's engagement after this mini project. Later, the class set themselves building-brain goals and his was 'Think harder, work faster'.

A self-evaluative mindset demands a relentless curiosity about finding new ways to turn on the brains of your pupils, meaning we will always be learning about learning. Keep up to date with the latest research that may inform your practice. Scan through the teacher's press and the Twitter teaching community, where you can link up with teachers' blogs about their current practice and join in with discussion forums. This is a truly invaluable continuing professional development (CPD) tool, offering something to learn and try out every week. At the end of the year, write your own self-evaluation document. Start by asking all the learners to feed back to you on your teaching. You could use sticky notes and have a board labelled 'Keep, Change, Grow', where pupils place their comments under each heading. They may suggest you cancel homework – but that will make a great class debate about what might help them achieve the best results. The very best teachers sustain a continuous dialogue with pupils about what they are learning and how they are learning it by using a suggestions board or box.

A pupil learning log can provide an invaluable and informative tool for teachers to browse through, and has the added bonus that it nurtures a language for learning in your pupils that becomes second nature (see pages

52–60). It develops their ability to think about learning and how it works. The process of metacognition gets you and your learners to step back and consider what is working and why – so that together you can make it work better and better over time. If it's working, stick with it; if it isn't, change it – especially if your pupils tell you so!

It really is in your own interest to reflect on and gather evidence of your impact. It can be useful for appraisal and applying for new posts or promotions as it provides evidence of how you adapt and respond over time.

Self-evaluation also includes becoming aware of your state of mind and body. So be sure to look after yourself through exercise, healthy eating and making time to meditate or relax.

Finally, visualise your lessons going well, not just superficially so, but imagine yourself becoming the best teacher – and learner – in the school!

TOP TIPS

- Ask your pupils for feedback on your teaching – regularly.

- Evaluate your everyday practice in a non-judgemental way by asking: 'What did I learn from that?' and 'What amendments can I make to get a better result?'

- Seek and soak up all the feedback you can get. If it is critical, try to consciously not blame yourself or others – just decide what you are going to do about it.

- Take advantage of every lesson observation (from leaders, inspectors or pupils) as an opportunity to learn. Request feedback. Make notes and learn from it.

- Take time out to reflect on how you are thinking and feeling on a regular basis.

- Remind yourself that your feelings are created by thoughts and that your brain can exaggerate, generalise and predict in unhelpful ways.

- Practise the process of metacognition to combat those brain tricks. Distance yourself from the emotional impact of your thinking sometimes. Challenge your thinking with the truth.

- Use meditation, mindfulness and exercise for a healthy mind and body.

- Mentally rehearse your next challenging lesson going well. During this, remind yourself of your core principles and beliefs about why you came into this profession.

BEHAVIOUR 2: BELIEVE THAT YOU CAN MAKE A DIFFERENCE

'I know that what I do in the classroom can have a big impact on a child's potential – no matter what their starting point.'

The most important thing you can do to be an outstanding teacher is to realise and believe that you *can* make a difference. A teacher's belief about how much they can influence outcomes has the greatest impact on pupils. (This doesn't, however, absolve the pupils from their contribution and responsibility!)

Reflect on how far you believe in the following statements:

- You are a change agent.

- High expectations are essential and children can always achieve more than we think.

- It is important to teach varied learning strategies to all pupils so that they can access their learning potential.

- Pupils who understand what progress looks like in your subject will make more of it because they are more capable of self-assessment and self-adjustment.

- Peer learning and peer teaching are powerful for learning.

- Making mistakes and being able to take critical feedback are crucial for improving learning.

- The challenges presented by poverty, parenting, prejudice, social class and home or school resources are surmountable.

The more you can embed these beliefs, the greater your impact as a teacher will be.

Your core values, and the reasons why you became a teacher, will help motivate and inspire you to become the best teacher you can be. According to Hattie, the conviction that you are a 'change agent', that you can make a difference because you believe that the outcomes for all children are not fixed, but influenced by us, is crucial to successful teaching.[5] He quotes from Alfieri, confirming

---

5   Hattie, *Visible Learning for Teachers*, p. 162.

research findings that teachers need to direct discovery through 'feedback, worked examples, scaffolding and elicited explanation' as activators of learning.[6] This places a high emphasis on the moral aspect of teaching. The best teachers have a mission, and it drives their practice, meaning that they intervene with their pupils to help them become great learners.

Most teachers believe that passing exams is important, but that using the skills and knowledge gained at school to become a successful human being and citizen is the greater goal of education. The teacher who believes that this is the job they are meant to do – helping every child learn and make progress without limits – will be building the bedrock of powerful teaching.

When you educate someone, you are changing their brain. That's what education is.

SARAH-JAYNE BLAKEMORE[7]

6   L. Alfieri, P. J. Brooks, N. J. Aldrich and H. R. Tenenbaum, Does Discovery-Based Instruction Enhance Learning?, *Journal of Educational Psychology* 103(1) (2011): 1-18, at 12.

7   Quoted in J. Lee, Open Your Mind to the Teachings of Neuroscience, *Times Educational Supplement* (1 March 2013). Available at: https://wwwtes.com/news/open-your-mind-teachings-neuroscience.

BEHAVIOUR 3: BE ENDLESSLY CURIOUS ABOUT LEARNING

How can I help my pupils remember the hard stuff? What made that strategy work so well this week? Why were my class so disengaged today? What is it that will help that quiet child make a breakthrough?

This third behaviour is about having an endless fascination with learning – how it works and why it works (or doesn't). For learners who struggle, the worst thing that can happen in their schooling is that teachers keep doing the same things in the same unsuccessful ways – over and over again – and expect a different result. Schools that constantly reflect on what works and what doesn't work in the classroom create a *mindset of enquiry* that means they are always learning about learning.

> *The best schools obsess about improving teaching.*
>
> **SUSAN GREGORY**[8]

The best teachers need to be endlessly flexible in their approaches to teaching and assessment, attending closely to feedback and responses to continually adjust and amend their plans, so that each child can make good progress.

---

8   S. Gregory, National Director Education and Early Years Introduces the Schools Report 2011/12 [video] (27 November 2012). Available at: https://webarchive.nationalarchives.govuk/video/Ofstednews/dFhCvzoBYM8.

THE GREATEST LEARNING MACHINE ON EARTH.

In Year 9, some bottom-set English classes are learning to improve their literacy and communication skills, in the same way that they did in Year 4 – and Years 5, 6, 7 and 8 ... No wonder they're turned off school, believe they're stupid and are bored out of their heads!

ENGLISH TEACHER

To become a 'learning expert', you need to obsess about learning. You have the perfect opportunity to do that every day as you observe your pupils growing their brains, adapting their skills, making connections and deepening their learning under your guidance. Develop a mindset that never stops puzzling over what works best and why – just like you did as a baby! Try learning a new language or skill and remind yourself just how vulnerable it makes you feel to struggle. What makes you stick at it? What helps you make progress?

It also helps to remind your struggling pupils that they once showed – and still have – these attributes!

TOP TIPS

- Keep a learning log. List things you would like to try, new words, comments you overhear from children or inspirational words you can share.

- Every day, try something new and note what you learn from it. Notice how you learn new skills and unlearn old ones. Become aware of when you go into autopilot and stop focusing on the details that make your teaching work brilliantly.

- Carry out some informal action research, maybe on an individual pupil or a class activity. Keep a note in your learning log, share it on Twitter, on your blog or deliver an INSET on the outcomes. Start a debate to extend the enquiry.

- Talk formally and informally to your classes to get feedback about your lessons. Look for trends and gather ideas for developing your teaching techniques.

- Visit other classrooms as often as possible and note anything positive, negative or interesting in your learning log.

- Engage in dialogue, not monologue, with your pupils so that you give them a chance to develop their thinking around the topic and they give you a chance to actively listen to how their learning is developing.

- Note the latest techniques used in social media, television programmes and advertising to intrigue and inform us. Adapt and use some of them in your lessons.

BEHAVIOUR 4: KNOW THAT FEEDBACK IS THE BREAKFAST OF CHAMPIONS

'I really prioritise giving and getting great feedback to grow my skills and help my pupils make more progress.'

Feedback is a powerful learning tool. The Sutton Trust[9] and the Education Endowment Foundation[10] found that feedback and metacognition made the most difference in closing the gap for disadvantaged children. So, how can we make it work for us in the classroom? How can we give feedback that motivates and really enhances progress?

We know that the home background and parenting of pupils will make this job harder or easier, but, in the time that they are with us, we need to teach pupils how to be great learners. We can do this by providing very regular written and oral feedback that helps them understand how they are doing and how they can do better – then making sure they act on our advice. The power of feedback is in the response it elicits.

Assessment provides an opportunity to feed back to pupils on their progress. Have they got it or not? If not, why not? What can I do differently to ensure that they do? How can I assess it and really know that they have learned it? Feedback is the crucial nourishment for progress.

Crucially, this mindset is also about realising that assessing and feeding back on pupils' progress assesses our own impact too, and is vital for self-evaluation (behaviour 1). The

---

9   S. Higgins, D. Kokotsaki and R. J. Coe, *Toolkit of Strategies to Improve Learning: Summary for Schools Spending the Pupil Premium* (London: Sutton Trust, 2011).

10 See https://educationendowmentfoundation.org.uk/evidence-summaries/teaching-learning-toolkit/feedback/.

best teachers accept that results reflect their teaching ability – even when the class is lazy or naughty. We want pupils to take responsibility for their own progress and outcomes; the tricky thing is acknowledging that developing pupil's independence and self-motivation is *our* responsibility.

The most important points about feedback are: first, you seek it out and, second, *you do something about it*. Adjust and calibrate on a minute-by-minute, hourly, daily and weekly basis. Make mistakes, take advice, discuss, share with colleagues and try something different. It is an iterative process and a continuous learning experience.

If you listen to feedback, discuss it with the pupils and then act on it, imagine how well you will be demonstrating to them that you too are a learner for life: that you are willing to take critical feedback, grow what is working well and change what isn't. And how much better is it to know what they (and your line managers) think than to carry on in ignorance?

TOP TIPS

- Help pupils constantly adjust by coaching and prompting them to assess their progress.

- Rename 'marking' as 'feedback' and make its purpose to help you know how pupils are progressing and actively help them improve.

- Use coaching questions to promote thinking – for example, 'What could you do next to help you move on?', 'How could this be even better?', 'Is there any way you would do this differently next time?' and 'What did you do last time that worked?' (See Chapter 7 for more on peer coaching.)

- Use a variety of low-stakes tests, quizzes, assessments and other progress checks to review knowledge and enhance memory.

- Reward effort and *value* responses to feedback by sharing high-quality examples with the class.

- Ensure the pupils are trained in peer-assessment techniques and peer critique that gives specific and helpful advice.

- Give opportunities for accurate, guided self-assessment so you encourage the same metacognitive habits that work for you.

- Present a range of strategies for learning and thinking in different ways and encourage the pupils to evaluate what works for them.

- Get feedback from pupils and line managers so that you can self-evaluate.

BEHAVIOUR 5: EXPECT MORE OF PUPILS (AND YOURSELF) BY TAKING RISKS

'I know that my pupils can always achieve more than I think they can.'

Constant changes in government policy, school systems, the national curriculum and examinations – not to mention the rise of the digital age and learning through social media – means teaching has never been more challenging.

Adapting to change is not optional but *essential* to ensure you can be a great teacher for the 21st century. If you love challenge, change and risk, you are open to the possibility that the children might know more than you and that children are capable of so much more than we ever could have imagined. Do you believe that pupils:

● Know more than we think they do?

● Can achieve more than their targets suggest?

● Will constantly surprise us with their sensitivity and maturity when we give them added responsibility?

Entering a classroom and expecting to be surprised by how much your pupils will achieve means you will always have the highest expectations and will communicate this to them. This may seem idealistic and, of course, some children will find things hard. But in the same way that a healthy baby never considers the possibility of failing to learn to walk or talk – no matter how long it takes and how many times they fall over – a great teacher doesn't see failure as an option. If it doesn't work then you try another way, and if that doesn't work, you try another way, and if that doesn't work, you try yet another way – until it works.

Pupils who catch this growth mindset from their teachers believe that the learning never ends. Teachers who do their best but think they know the limitations of their pupils are destined to settle for mediocrity.

J. K. Rowling struggled with years of failure before she found fame with the Harry Potter novels. She famously said:

> *It is impossible to live without failing at something, unless you live so cautiously that you may as well not have lived at all.*[11]

This challenge – to believe that anything is possible – is huge and scary for both teachers and pupils. Teachers need to know that it is alright to risk teaching new strategies and to share with pupils that they too are on a learning journey. Pupils need to know that learning can be hard, painful, boring, repetitive, frustrating, that it risks failure (and that this is part of the process) and can also be fun and fascinating. The best teachers know how to get their pupils into the challenging terrain outside of their comfort zones, with the help of unconditional support from their peers. As pupils learn to do this and enjoy it, they learn that through taking risks they can expect to do more, and the learning becomes less scary.

Risk-taking is essential for learners if they are going to make maximum progress. Trying harder activities, reading difficult texts, solving 'impossible' problems and learning to play that complex piece of music are the types of challenge that make pupils start to acquire the habits of persistence and resilience that they need in order to be successful. Although nature seems to knock spots off nurture in terms of defining how intelligent we are, the research shows that it's the opportunities to choose to grow these habits that makes the biggest difference.[12]

---

11 J. K. Rowling, The Fringe Benefits of Failure, and the Importance of Imagination. Speech delivered at the Harvard University Commencement (5 June 2008). Transcript available at: https://news.harvard.edu/gazette/story/2008/06/text-of-j-k-rowling-speech/.

12 Willingham, *Why Don't Children Like School?*, p. 178.

We've all had rubbish lessons where everything went wrong and maybe we lost control or forgot some key points at the crucial moment. We've all said something stupid or had a bad set of results at some point. I've made mistakes both as a teacher and a leader and as I look back, I know they made me more vulnerable and more resilient in equal measure.

HEAD TEACHER

A job isn't worth doing if it isn't scary.

JASMINE WHITBREAD[13]

USE HOMEWORK TO STOKE FIRES

Making homework a highly effective learning experience is a constant challenge for all teachers. The very best teachers will set challenging work that extends learning beyond the lesson, not just as a bolt-on to please parents. Motivating pupils to enjoy 'home learning' by applying their schoolwork to extended projects or 'flipping classrooms' (see Chapter 3) – so that they learn at home, then use that learning in lessons – may offer great opportunities to challenge your class. Willingham says that 'whatever students think about, is what they will remember'.[14] The challenge, then, is to make homework a problem to solve, or a challenge to undertake, that will make pupils think about what they need to remember for next lesson. This could be anything from learning a passage of Shakespeare by heart to creating a mind map of the what, why, how,

---

13 Jasmine Whitbread, CEO of Save the Children, *Woman's Hour*, BBC Radio 4, 31 July 2013.

14 Willingham, *Why Don't Children Like School?*, p. 54.

where and when details of the lesson taught today to deepen the learning.

TOP TIPS

- Make 'High challenge, maximum peer support' one of your classroom mantras. A classroom culture of allies is the ultimate climate for good progress for all.[15] When we all support each other, we don't mind taking risks for learning. (See behaviour 6.)

- Believe that all pupils innately have the resources to make good progress – we just need to find the right strategy.

- Take risks. If learning doesn't go well, don't blame yourself or the kids – just adapt what you are doing until it works better.

- Encourage the pupils to have high expectations of themselves by establishing a culture that understands that learning requires hard work. Ensure they know that if they aren't feeling challenged, then they aren't growing their brains.

- Set homework that is motivating, extends learning and makes it connect with the lives of your pupils.

- Approach every lesson expecting the pupils to surprise you with what they *can* do. When they struggle, tell them how good it is that they are growing new neural pathways. This will make them more intelligent if they keep trying.

---

15 Dweck, *Mindset*.

BEHAVIOUR 6:
COLLABORATE TO GROW

'I always take regular opportunities to work with colleagues outside my subject or phase and I always learn something new from it.'

Collaboration and interdependency – teacher with teacher and pupil with pupil – are powerful. They synergise connections and learning so people make more progress together. If we adopt this as a principle in our working life – and we share ideas, resources, strategies and problems – it will maximise our impact as teachers. Not only that, we will improve our own communication skills to become better networkers and be more popular, charismatic and influential!

What happens when you help someone else to improve? Do you benefit when you give time and energy to support someone else in their learning journey and it works? Have you learned anything from helping someone else overcome a challenge?

Apart from the feel-good factor, 'the effects of peers on learning is high' (effect size of 0.52), especially if a culture of trust and aspiration is embedded in the classroom.[16] When we teach, we learn. When children teach each other, they can deepen their understanding and secure their knowledge. (Providing we check they're teaching correctly!)

Does your class know how powerful collaboration is? Do you train them to communicate effectively so that they can make the most of working in groups and teams? Taking on various team roles, giving and receiving feedback, discussing, debating and negotiating solutions to

---

16 Hattie, *Visible Learning for Teachers,* p. 87.

problems are all activities that will build those essential collaborative skills.

Imagine if, in your classroom, every pupil gave unconditional support to others to help them make the maximum progress. Pupils would be unafraid to ask and answer questions, would take more risks and would improve their progress. Teachers who believe it is a major part of their role to develop positive relationships in classrooms and staffrooms know that those who 'fire together, wire together', and thereby create powerful learning communities.

TOP TIPS

- Work with your colleagues to plan, teach and assess together as often as possible.

- Get yourself a peer coach and peer coach a colleague – at least once a half term (see Chapter 7).

- Habitually share resources, ideas and strategies (and problems!) with colleagues.

- Get involved in working parties, training events and extracurricular days as often as possible.

- In your classes and department, establish zero tolerance of put-downs and big rewards for showing unconditional support for learning and progress.

- Value collaborative learning in your classroom.

- Encourage talking, planning and thinking in structured and unstructured ways.

- Improve communication skills by encouraging opportunities for public speaking, performing and debating.

- Make pupils teaching each other a key element of your planning and practice.

BEHAVIOUR 7: USE A LANGUAGE FOR LEARNING

'We talk about learning with pupils and parents so they can understand how to help create new learning strategies and solutions.'

The best teachers say: 'I am passionate about and promote the language of learning.'[17]

Learning is a process that happens invisibly inside our heads. Making learning a conscious, visible process requires a language for learning. It needs a vocabulary that pupils can use to discuss and debate the process of learning and communicate how it works for them. Teaching pupils to reflect on and be able to communicate what they have learned (or not) and how (or why not) starts to make the learning process more visible for them.

This fits with Rosenshine's helpful principles of instruction, which are based on cognitive and classroom practice research.[18] He suggests that the best teachers 'think out loud' and provide models that clarify specific steps to learning. This gives pupils the cognitive support and, I

---

17 Hattie, *Visible Learning for Teachers*, p. 6.
18 B. Rosenshine, Principles of Instruction: Research-Based Strategies That All Teachers Should Know, *American Educator* 36(1) (2012): 12–19, 39.

would argue, the language they need to become good learners.

Many professions have a language that defines their activity and encourages debate and discussion about strategies. Giving teachers and parents a language to help them talk to their children about their learning has led to enhanced engagement by students in their schooling experiences. Hattie stresses in his research that when parents learned the language about the nature of learning in classrooms it helped their children 'attend and engage in learning'.[19]

Which of these words describe learning for you and your pupils?

Thinking. Creating. Remembering. Considering. Imagining. Deciding. Choosing. Hypothesising. Rehearsing. Studying. Swotting. Absorbing. Understanding. Drafting. Practising. Listening. Speaking. Connecting. Reading. Writing. Questioning. Seeing. Hearing. Feeling. Tasting. Touching.

The best teachers develop pupils who can communicate how to improve their work and have high levels of engagement and commitment to learning, alongside resilience and independence. To achieve this, these teachers regularly use a language for learning to share success criteria, helping learners understand exactly what they need to do to improve. As a result, pupils are better able to discuss and track their progress and address their weaknesses with more understanding, confidence and courage.

---

19 Hattie, *Visible Learning for Teachers*, p. 188.

Pupils with a language for learning better understand the terms used in and the purpose of feedback and constructive criticism, becoming more self-motivated and able to debate their progress. Pupils (and teachers!) who can dispassionately describe their own and each other's work against success criteria are better able to take criticism because they understand that its purpose is to help them move forward. Feedback becomes information, not judgement. The more we practise taking valid criticism and learning from it, the more we become the hungry, resilient learners we need to be to thrive.

If pupils can talk about a variety of learning strategies, they are usually better at spotting mistakes and seeing them as an opportunity to learn – not as a symptom of failure. When pupils can talk about the way in which they learn, it helps them to take more control of and responsibility for their own progress. (As Daniel Willingham says, 'Praising process rather than ability sends the unspoken message that intelligence is under the student's control.'[20]) A language for learning makes it easier for pupils to understand that learned helplessness and dependency are the result if they are towed through tests by the teacher. They will also learn the meaning of resilience and the ability to learn by themselves, for themselves, to deliver lifelong learning skills.[21]

Features of a growth mindset language for learning include:

- A change from a 'judge and be judged' to a 'learn and help learn' mindset.

- Language which praises processes and effort and avoids judging or defining ability.

---

20 Willingham, *Why Don't Students Like School?*, p. 183.

21 K. Wall, E. Hall, V. Baumfield, et al., *Learning to Learn in School Phase 4 and Learning to Learn in Further Education* (London: Campaign for Learning, 2010).

- Pupils use language such as: effort, goals, practice, coach, support, objective, metacognition, feedback, develop, create, collaborate, resilience, learn, grow, challenge, connections, reflect, review, consider and communicate.

- Pupils are able to respond eloquently to questions such as:

  ▲ 'What did that mistake or setback teach you today?'

  ▲ 'Can you describe the thinking that helped you work that out?'

  ▲ And if they're struggling, 'What strategies can you use to do that better?'

The formula for successful schooling involves teachers becoming more aware of their impact so that the pupil becomes the teacher and the teacher becomes the learner. This also requires a shared language for learning. (See Chapter 7 for more details.)

Teachers who instil a love of their subject and a desire to know more in their learners are the teachers we remember. They communicate their passion and the subject material clearly in terms that the pupils understand, constantly connecting and calibrating their approach and language. Pupils are then more likely to mirror the teacher's enthusiasm and passion and tackle the challenges of learning with more resilience and interest.

> *Passion reflects the thrill, as well as the frustrations, of learning; it can be infectious, it can be taught, it can be modelled, and it can be learnt.*
>
> **JOHN HATTIE**[22]

However, learners need to do more than know stuff, they need to be able to challenge ideas and apply what they learn to new situations, as Peter C. Brown et al. remind us in *Make It Stick*:

> *The illusion of mastery is a poor example of metacognition ... when they have reread their lecture notes and texts to the point of fluency. Their fluency gives them the false sense that they are in possession of the underlying content, principles and implications that constitute real learning.*[23]

There needs to be real progress in understanding and knowledge in your lessons. When your teaching is appraised, can your pupils express:

- What they are learning in your lessons and why?

- How they are learning?

- How it links to other areas of learning?

- What they need to do next?

Pupils who have the language needed to express their reflections on learning can better articulate the learning intentions in their own words and comment on the wider context and purpose of the lesson, as this example illustrates.

---

22 Hattie, *Visible Learning for Teachers*, p. 16.

23 P. C. Brown, H. L. Roediger and M. A. McDaniel, *Make It Stick: The Science of Successful Learning* (Cambridge, MA: The Belknap Press, 2014), pp. 16–17.

Ofsted inspector: Why are you learning about volcanoes?

Answer 1: Don't know really. I suppose it's because we've got to do it in science.

Answer 2: Because they're important in forming new igneous rocks, are dangerous for people living near them and put lots of CO_2 into the air. This means they're linked to global warming and to what we did about plate tectonics and to the stuff we did about human geography and the earth's history, and extinctions … Want to know how?

How a pupil answers a question can tell us so much about the way in which they have been taught and whether or not they can reflect on the nuances of meaning, rather than recite the facts.

Some parents spend lots of time talking to their children from the moment they are born. They run a descriptive narrative of the world around their growing children, allowing them to accumulate a much richer, more expansive vocabulary than some of their peers by the time they reach school age.

Because they have had their why, what, when and how questions answered, not rebuffed, these children keep asking and wondering and thinking and learning. By the age of 7, the destiny of many of these pupils has been substantially programmed by their ability to have a dialogue about the things they learn. (You can see this by watching the classic 1964 television programme *Seven Up!*[24]) Some

---

24 *Seven Up!*, Granada Television (1964). Available at: https://www.youtube.com/watch?v=1LQZpiSfESE.

children don't benefit from a family life that promotes debate and discussion about their learning in school. An excellent teacher will work hard with such children to develop this language for learning and help them close the gap in achievement – a gap which will continue to widen unless they can think and talk about how they learn.

DELIBERATELY DEVELOP A LANGUAGE FOR LEARNING WITH YOUR UNDERACHIEVERS

Your impact as a teacher will be judged by how your pupils achieve, and particularly by how you help to improve the outcomes of those who are not making enough progress. Make sure you talk regularly to pupils who have additional needs, or who are lagging behind. Help them to develop a language for learning and useful learning strategies that will embed the content and enhance their understanding. (See Chapter 6 for more tips.)

If your pupils are used to talking about their learning, and have the vocabulary to describe it, they will be able to accurately explain how they are making progress to any-one who cares to ask. However, without knowing how to talk and think about learning and how it works, your vul-nerable learners will always be behind the starting line in lessons. Make sure that any TAs who work with these chil-dren are giving them effective strategies for independent learning. They are vital allies in supporting children's think-ing habits. TAs can transform the potential of any disadvantaged child or entrench their expectation of fail-ure. This is a very good reason why we need effective training for TAs.

TOP TIPS

- Engage the pupils in the learning intentions/ outcomes/objectives or whatever you call them.

- Make sure they know the wider context of the learning and its relevance to their everyday lives.

- Include problem-solving challenges in your curriculum and get pupils to understand how they can apply their learning to these challenges.

- Talk about the 'how' of learning as well as the 'what' in every lesson.

- Involve pupils in the process and planning.

- Give your pupils useful vocabulary to describe both their subject- and skills-based learning experiences. Check they aren't just echoing back to you, but really get it.

- When a child gets something right, ask them to explain their thinking and how they worked it out for everyone to hear. This encourages metacognition.

- Encourage peer assessment and peer feedback that uses a language for learning.

- Help them to understand that learning is a journey.

- Get the pupils to design posters about learning to display in classrooms.

- Lay down a philosophy for developing the habits of great learning that includes words such as optimism, empathy, support, resilience, determination, curiosity, creativity, collaboration and enquiry.

- Give pupils rewards for demonstrating these qualities and reinforce them by recognising and commenting on them.

- Run a learning-to-learn programme for your TAs and pupils. Encourage them to develop individual learning strategies that work.

- Complete the growth mindset health check (see Appendix 2) to set yourself targets and help you put these mindsets into practice every day.

'There is nothing either good or bad, but thinking makes it so.'

WILLIAM SHAKESPEARE, *HAMLET*, **ACT 2, SCENE 2**

CHAPTER 3

HOW TO DELIVER A GREAT LESSON

The most important thing you do as a teacher is deliver great lessons as often as possible. Every teacher prepares their best lessons differently. Many schools have a tick list for 'outstanding lessons', but anyone who has ever observed a lesson knows that there is much more to it than following a to-do list. So much is dependent on the mindset and the unconscious messages delivered by the teacher – hence all the information in the first two chapters! There is no one magic formula or set structure for the 'perfect' lesson, but the ideas here will help you to develop your own version of the very best learning experiences for your class, every day.

How can you ensure that your pupils 'typically' make great progress and achieve their full potential? By establishing a culture that embeds the behaviours of great learners. I've identified seven essential steps to delivering your best lessons every day.

STEP 1: KNOW WHAT WORKS AND WHAT MAKES A GREAT TEACHER

This summary of effective habits and behaviours – as described in Ofsted's grade descriptors for 'outstanding' over recent years (some quoted, others summarised by me) – makes a good starting point:

- They plan lessons very effectively, making maximum use of lesson time and building towards a goal.

- They manage pupils' behaviour highly effectively with clear rules that are consistently enforced.

- Teachers demonstrate deep knowledge and understanding of the subjects they teach.

- They use questioning highly effectively and demonstrate an understanding of the ways in which pupils think about subject content, identifying pupils' common misconceptions and acting to ensure that they are corrected and committed to long-term memory.

- Teachers provide adequate time for practice to embed the pupils' knowledge, understanding and skills securely. They introduce subject content progressively and constantly demand more of pupils.

- Teachers identify and support any pupil who is falling behind, checking pupils' understanding systematically and effectively in lessons, offering clearly directed and timely support.

- Teachers provide pupils with incisive feedback, in line with the school's assessment policy, showing what pupils can do to improve their knowledge, understanding and skills. The pupils use this feedback effectively to develop their understanding.

- Teachers set challenging homework, in line with the school's policy, appropriate for the age and stage of pupils, that consolidates learning, deepens understanding and prepares pupils very well for work to come.

- Teachers embed reading, writing, communication and, where appropriate, mathematics exceptionally well across the curriculum, equipping all pupils with the necessary skills to make progress. For younger children in particular, phonics teaching is highly effective in enabling them to tackle unfamiliar words.

- Teachers are determined that pupils achieve well. They encourage pupils to try hard, recognise their efforts and ensure that pupils take pride in all aspects of their work by having consistently high expectations of all pupils' attitudes to learning.

- Resources and teaching strategies reflect and value the diversity of pupils' experiences and provide pupils with a comprehensive understanding of people and communities beyond their immediate experience.

- Teachers ensure that their speaking, listening, writing and reading skills are appropriate and support pupils in developing their language and vocabulary well.

- Teachers provide parents with clear and timely information on how well their child is progressing and how well their child is doing in relation to the standards expected. Parents are given guidance about how to support their child to improve.

All these behaviours work to develop great teaching over time and nurture pupils who:

- Are eager to know how to improve their learning and who always use feedback, written or oral, to improve.

- Love the challenge of learning and are resilient to failure. They become curious, interested learners who seek out and use new information to develop, consolidate and deepen their knowledge, understanding and skills. They thrive in lessons and regularly take up opportunities to learn through extracurricular activities.

The one-off brilliant lesson when you are being observed is satisfying, but it is impact over time that counts. When talking to pupils and looking at the work they produce, the quality of the teaching over time will soon become clear. This is why individual teachers or lessons are no longer graded by Ofsted. They are looking for 'typicality' across the whole school culture. This is a very good reason to make sure that what you are delivering each and every day is helping children to progress and remember what they have learned and how to apply it.

Simple measures of progress: knowing more, remembering more, doing more.[1]

What are the magic ingredients that will make your teaching outstanding and demonstrate the high quality of provision in your school?

Some key ingredients for success, based on the descriptors listed are:

- All the pupils, particularly those who have the greatest needs, are making rapid and sustained progress in learning and applying this learning to new situations.

- Able children experience opportunities to really challenge themselves and fulfil their potential.

1   This is an adapted version of 'Progress, therefore, means knowing more (including knowing how to do more) and remembering more', taken from Ofsted, Education Inspection Framework 2019: Inspecting the Substance of Education [Consultation outcome] (29 July 2019). Available at: https://www.gov.uk/government/consultations/education-inspection-framework-2019-inspecting-the-substance-of-education/education-inspection-framework-2019-inspecting-the-substance-of-education.

- Teachers have very high expectations of all pupils and enable them to learn exceptionally well across the curriculum, and this includes modelling and promoting the core skills of literacy and numeracy in all subjects.

- Teachers are constantly checking understanding, giving powerful feedback and intervening with impact on pupils' progress and learning. Pupils are responding to the feedback given and consequently making more progress.

- Imaginative teaching strategies are used to engage and motivate pupils on a regular basis – not just for observations – evidenced by their positive attitude to learning.

- Teachers are sharing the criteria for success to enable pupils to have ownership of and commitment to their own learning.

Personal development is now a key judgement in evaluating schools, so every lesson should include a focus on:

- Developing independent and resilient learners.

- Using classroom assistants effectively so that they can help the neediest pupils make exceptional progress in the lesson.

- Assessment being used as an integral part of developing progress in learning. Children's work will demonstrate this and show how they respond to feedback and that they are willing to learn from mistakes.

- Challenging the most able learners to really work to their full potential.

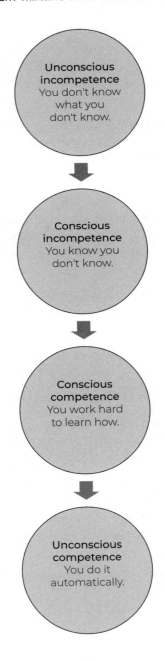

- Understanding the opportunities and dangers of using technology and social media.

- Effective collaborative learning and peer critique.

- Developing behaviour and attitudes that enhance learning for all by creating a culture of allies.

How can you demonstrate all this? First, you need to be aware. Then take Willingham's advice: 'Your best bet for improving your teaching is to practice teaching'.[2] These skills will develop over time until they become unconscious and habitual and 'just the way you teach'. You'll become unconsciously competent (see figure on page 66).[3]

However, the journey towards unconscious competence is beset by periods of conscious incompetence and lots of hard work! Admit to and learn from your mistakes then adapt, improvise, adjust and improve. Be relentless in your efforts to improve your practice, grow the pupils' intelligence and improve achievement for all.

Based on decades of cognitive science research and evidence from successful classroom practice, Barak Rosenshine established his principles of instruction.[4] The main takeaways from his common-sense guidance is to teach in small steps, review regularly, and include lots of guided practice and great questioning to give you feedback on what your pupils really know and understand. This should underpin everyday teaching.

Over time, if you establish a classroom culture in which learning is truly valued, and high expectations of yourself

---

2 Willingham, *Why Don't Students Like School?*, p. 191.
3 This model is thought to have its origins in Martin M. Broadwell's work on levels of learning: Teaching for Learning (XVI), *The Gospel Guardian* (20 February 1969). Available at: http://wwwwordsfitlyspoken.org/gospel_guardian/v20/v20n41p1-3a.html.
4 Rosenshine, Principles of Instruction.

and others are habitual, then anyone walking into your lesson will immediately know that you are a highly effective teacher. This will be clear by seeing how keen the children are to *self-test and peer test* to show how much they have learned and how determined they are to fill in any gaps in their learning. Make sure that your pupils always feel free to chat about what happens in your classroom – they are the best advocates of your teaching and will be keen to explain how you help them learn! The following chapters will give you much more detail about how to achieve this ideal classroom culture. However, first we'll consider the remaining steps.

STEP 2: BE PRESENT AND IN CONTROL, RIGHT FROM THE START

Demonstrate this every day by displaying that same thirst for knowledge and love of learning that we expect to see from the pupils. Teachers who are open to new ideas – who learn from colleagues, pupils and their mistakes – and nurture excellent attitudes to learning will always have a strong, positive impact on pupils' progress.

Also, train your pupils to coach each other (and themselves) to keep trying, even when they get stuck or make mistakes. If you can develop this habit of resilience in your lessons, it will shine through in every conversation any inspector or observer may have with your pupils. An excellent way to create this culture is to share how you yourself bounce back from mistakes.

There is nothing more inspiring than for someone in a position of power to show humility by admitting they are wrong, or scared, or not sure – and that this is OK. Vulnerability makes us stronger, not weaker.

CLASSROOM LEADERSHIP ROLES

Choose a pupil to be your lead greeter. Their job is to welcome any visitor to the classroom and, using a copy of your lesson plan, be able to help the visitor see what progress you have made so far in the lesson – and how you have made it. Other roles for your classroom can be lead questioner, lead celebrator, literacy ambassador, growth mindset guru, etc. (see more examples in Appendix 1) – all are intended to give pupils responsibilities that challenge them out of their comfort zone and support your classroom culture of high expectations for all.

Rosenshine et al. commented on the vital role of regular review in deepening learning.[5] So why not have another leadership role of quizmaster or knowledge checker? During a lesson they could prepare quick questions or a cloze (missing words) exercise on the content to be used to review learning at the beginning of the next lesson.

SET UP THE LEARNING ENVIRONMENT

Be there to greet the pupils by name as they arrive. Always make a prompt start – especially for early arrivers. Get the pupils into the habit of self-starting in every lesson by setting little challenges, questions or tasks that they *know* they are expected to get on with immediately. These can

---

5   B. Rosenshine, C. Meister and S. Chapman, Teaching Students to Generate Questions: A Review of Intervention Studies, *Review of Educational Research* 66 (1996): 181–221.

be anagrams, puzzles, true or false statements, recaps of the previous lesson(s), unexpected questions for debate, music challenges and so on. The aim is to intrigue and engage while connecting and embedding previous learning. Reward effort for these tasks as part of your reward-and-sanction classroom policy. It neatly shows how you are completely and effortlessly in control and makes a great impression on that unexpected visitor who will see that your pupils are in the habit of starting learning as soon as they walk through your classroom door.

It can be a good idea to play music as pupils come in and get on with these tasks. (See Nina Jackson's excellent and aptly named book for some suggestions.[6]) Then, when you switch the music off, the pupils know it is time for the lesson proper to start.

While the pupils are completing the tasks, circulate, smile, greet them individually by name and make them feel welcome and valued. You could get the pupils to assess each other's work, if appropriate. You can then start the main part of the lesson when *you* are ready and useful work is already taking place.

The culture of the classroom is crucial to developing the good personal development habits expected of pupils. It will also make your life much easier if children walk into your classroom and unconsciously know the high standards of behaviour and effort that are expected. Being rigorous about boundaries for behaviour and following through with sanctions right from the start is the only way to create this culture. It also makes the pupils feel safe and more eager to learn, able to ask questions and to support each other unconditionally to make greater progress.

---

6 N. Jackson, *The Little Book of Music for the Classroom: Using Music to Improve Memory, Motivation, Learning and Creativity* (Carmarthen: Independent Thinking Press, 2009).

STEP 3: PLAN THE STARTER THAT PRIMES THEM FOR LEARNING – AND FINDS OUT WHAT THEY ALREADY KNOW

Your first learning activity should stimulate curiosity and open-mindedness and prepare the brain for learning. Engaging the emotional brain makes your class curious and attentive.

If there is no right or wrong answer to a starter question, it encourages a growth mindset attitude to learning and doesn't make a child feel judged or graded. This activity can sometimes be chosen at random or, better, linked to the subject to review prior learning.

Some suggestions for starters follow.

START WITH A THUNK

This is a question which has no right or wrong answer but which makes the pupils think. Thunks were created by Ian Gilbert, and a vast collection can be found in *The Little Book of Thunks*[7] and *The Compleat Thunks Book*[8]. Thunks prepare pupils to be open-minded and consider various options. Some random and some subject-linked examples follow.

> If you always got what you wished for would you always be happy?

---

7   I. Gilbert, *The Little Book of Thunks: 260 Questions to Make Your Brain Go Ouch!* (Carmarthen: Independent Thinking Press, 2007).

8   I. Gilbert, *The Compleat Thunks Book* (Carmarthen: Independent Thinking Press, 2017).

Which has the most freedom – an ant or a schoolchild?

Is a person who has a face transplant still the same person?

Which is heavier, an inflated or deflated balloon?

Is love invisible?

Can being sad make you happy?

Can you experience fear without being scared?

Pupils can think of the next question or make up their own Thunks as part of the starter. Linking these to your lesson topic is even better.

Here are a few more philosophical thinking questions that may suit a starter for maths or science:

How many sides does a line have?

If a plant isn't green, is it a plant?

If a machine is breathing for you, are you dead?

Is a maths answer always right or wrong?

Does a baked cake weigh more than its ingredients?

Does a circle have two sides?

Can you point to where the sky begins?

START WITH A CURIOSITY

You can make the curiosity link to your subject or the lesson:

● A box. The pupils have to guess what the contents are.

- A wig or hat. Someone can try it on and guess the character it belongs to.

- A message in a bottle. The pupils have to guess the message and who sent it.

- A tray of relevant items covered with a tea towel. The pupils have to guess what might be underneath based on the lesson topic or last week's lesson.

- A crime scene to investigate.

START WITH A CREATIVE CHALLENGE IN PAIRS

For example:

- List the three most popular babies' names today and create three names that could be popular in ten years' time.

- Guess the most common and least common food that people in the class had for breakfast.

- How could we use maths to create a better world?

- What genes would you change in humans to make us a better species?

- Think of three ways in which you can help to cure global warming/discover life on other planets/use geometry to redecorate your bedroom/teach a child how to use commas.

- Draw a logo, and write an accompanying slogan, that represents what we learned last lesson.

WORK FOR, PARTY WITH OR SEND TO THE JUNGLE

A fun task that helps pupils understand personal preferences. Give the pupils three famous names (choosing popular figures) and ask them who they would do what with and why.

For example:

- Prince William, Ed Sheeran, Nigel Farage.
- Cheryl, Caroline Flack, Fern Britton.
- Michael McIntyre, Boris Johnson, Adele.
- Donald Trump, William Shakespeare, Martin Luther King, Jr.
- Brian Cox, Charles Darwin, Marie Curie.

ROOM 101

This is the room full of your worst nightmares. For Winston in George Orwell's *1984* it was rats.

What three things would you put into Room 101 and why?

EMBED THE SKILLS FOR PERSONAL AND CAREER DEVELOPMENT AS PART OF YOUR STARTER ACTIVITY

Ensure that your pupils are developing the skills and attitudes to enable them to participate fully in and contribute positively to life in modern society by giving opportunities to reflect on and share their values and beliefs. Prime the learners in this by linking the lesson explicitly to one of the personal, learning and thinking skills (PLTs). In their day, these were identified as the key skills employers require for the workplace. Although this model is no longer part of the educational policy agenda, I still think that it provides us with a useful framework. Some examples of starter and other tasks involving these vital skills appear in the table that follows. Success could earn points that accumulate over time and gain rewards.

Personal, learning and thinking skills	Task
Self-manager	Draw a face that depicts the different moods you have experienced today so far
Effective participator	Write down five things you will do in this lesson to help others learn
Creative thinker	Design a logo and slogan for this subject/lesson
Reflective learner	Create a mind map of what we did last lesson
Independent enquirer	Write three questions you need to ask about what we did last lesson
Teamworker	Think of three promises you will make to your team to help it work well

Be energetic and enthusiastic about setting up these tasks. Check out the impact and show your pupils how important progress in the PLTs is for success. Channel any nerves into passion if you are being observed!

STEP 4: SET CLEAR OBJECTIVES AND SUCCESS CRITERIA, ENGAGING THEM IN THE LEARNING JOURNEY

What am I trying to achieve this lesson? How will I engage the pupils? How will I, and they, know that we've achieved it? These are the only questions that matter.

CLEAR OBJECTIVES

Your objective can be a skill to develop, a question to answer or some knowledge you are trying to help them acquire. It doesn't have to be set out at the beginning of every lesson, it doesn't have to be written in books, but it should be understood by all … 'Exactly what is it we are trying to learn?'

When you explain the objective, you should answer any questions pupils have – for example, 'What's in it for me?', 'What will I be able to do better after this?' and 'Why should I bother with this lesson?' If they can see *what* they are learning and *why,* it will help them engage. Explain the objectives in terms of the bigger picture: that is, how they relate to the last lesson's learning, the course they are following and the big overall goal. You can't simply write the objectives on the board and get the pupils to merely copy them down. This is a waste of time. Get the pupils to engage with your objectives so they are able to explain them and how their learning journey will develop.

Describing what the lesson is about is the crucial moment when you engage the pupils in the exciting task ahead and explain that it will make a difference to them personally.

To succeed, you must communicate your expectation of success and your personal excitement about the subject – what they can achieve and why it is important.

SUCCESS CRITERIA

Crucially, the success criteria for achieving the outcomes also need to be negotiated with and understood by the pupils for maximum engagement. If possible, share an example of a WAGOLL (What A Good One Looks Like) with them to enable them to be clear about what success will look, feel or sound like when they have made that progress.

Consider using differentiated objectives and differentiated success criteria. Be careful, though, that they don't cap the effort of, or outcome for, some pupils. (This can happen with the 'some/most/all students will ...' models). Everyone should aim for the highest outcome and aim to find a way to get there over time.

Aim high but be willing to adjust and adapt for individuals. Persistently communicate your high expectations and your determination to find the strategies to help them excel. Make sure specific groups of pupils are aware of what they need to do to make progress. Ensure that the most and least able, and vulnerable pupils, all have that extra bit of attention, resources or scaffolding to ensure that they know how to make progress. Doing this effectively shows that you and the other adults in the room are acutely aware of the pupils' capabilities and of their prior learning and that you plan very effectively to build on these. Minds grow when they are fed with optimism and hope for the future. Our children have to rely on their attitudes to save the world.

There's no need for lengthy typed lesson plans, but planning lessons that build upon prior learning and progress pupils' thinking is essential. (See Appendix 4 for a useful five-minute lesson plan.) Willingham suggests that you make the lesson plan into a story to help pupils remember it.[9] Bear in mind that any plan isn't rigid and that the lesson must respond to pupil feedback. Change tack if you need to. Review and repeat if they need you to – being flexible is the hallmark of a great teacher.

TOP TIPS

- Try to connect the lesson plan to something that resonates with your pupils' interests and values and connects with their prior learning.

- Describe simply and *exactly* what you want the pupils to be able to do or know by the end of the lesson.

- Teach to the top and intervene, anticipate and scaffold for those who need extra help to achieve their potential.

- Explain the success criteria.

- Even better, ask them to suggest what the success criteria could be and how they would know they have met them.

- Create a culture in your classroom in which all pupils are willing to push themselves outside of their comfort zones so that they can 'grow' their brains.

---

9   Willingham, *Why Don't Students Like School?*

● If possible, show an example of what a high-quality outcome looks like so they can see what they are aiming for. Talk about the learning journey involved and how mistakes along the way are inevitable and important for learning.

THE LEARNING JOURNEY

Return to the overall learning journey (periodically). It is important that the pupils know that this and previous lessons are part of a greater learning journey and that they have an amazing capacity to progress towards the overall aims. There are three steps to doing this:

1   Explaining (with passion) what success in achieving the objectives will look and feel like (i.e. the 'brilliant outcome' or WAGOLL).

2   Showing them that achieving the objectives is part of a learning journey towards a greater goal by using a continuum line, but explaining that the journey may involve challenges, mistakes and getting stuck – it's not just a straightforward, one-way trajectory.

3   By setting one or more personal skills objectives for individual (or targeted) pupils.

Draw a line that leads to the 'brilliant outcome' (WAGOLL) they are heading towards in their learning journey. During the activity pupils can decide where they are along the line. After the task they mark where they are now to demonstrate the progress they've made in the lesson(s) towards the overall outcome(s) in the objective and the PLTs (see page 80).

Objective: To recognise the power of different types of language

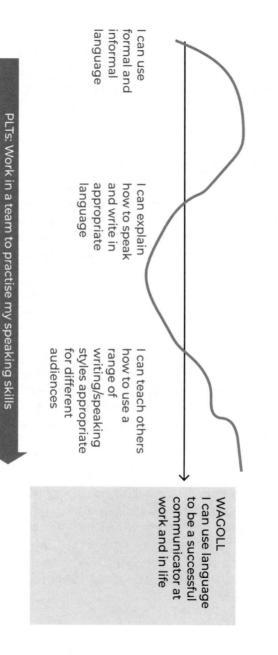

I can use formal and informal language

I can explain how to speak and write in appropriate language

I can teach others how to use a range of writing/speaking styles appropriate for different audiences

PLTs: Work in a team to practise my speaking skills

WAGOLL
I can use language to be a successful communicator at work and in life

You can also discuss what the challenges might be along the way, when they might get stuck and what strategies they could use to get 'unstuck'. This is a great opportunity to emphasise that learning is hardly ever a simple journey. Tell them to expect hard bits or that they might get lost, which might be frustrating, but with the right attitude and strategies they can overcome anything! Children who are encouraged to think in this growth mindset way love a challenge and know that struggle equals growth and that it can grow new neural pathways. Demonstrate the way learning works by dedicating some of your walls to showing the process.

A huge arrow across your classroom wall will enable you to talk to the whole class about how they have progressed in the lesson or series of lessons. Using sticky notes, you can show their progress along their learning journey as illustrated in the example on page 82.

Learning is never just linear, but if we are moving along towards our learning goals, we can become more aware of the process of learning and the cognitive connections required. Research has found that such a focus can make a profound difference to progress.[10]

STEP 5: DELIVER THE MAIN ACTIVITY (OR ACTIVITIES)

This is where the teacher's expertise really counts to facilitate the learning and maximise progress. In outstanding classrooms, pupils demonstrate that they can work well together or on their own. Varying your activities will develop the flexibility that all learners need and encourage

---

10 Wall, Hall, Baumfield, et al., *Learning to Learn*.

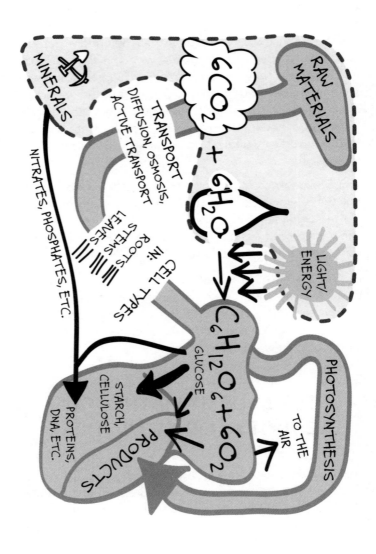

good learning habits so that pupils thrive in lessons and in learning at home.

In your classroom there needs to be:

- A challenging level of subject knowledge, a passion for the subject and an ability to communicate it in ways that enthuse the pupils and connect to prior knowledge.

- Active, collaborative learning – it is crucial to show that pupils can work on task, with or without adult supervision.

- A choice of challenging activities or approaches available. A chance to talk, teach each other and problem-solve with a focus on high-quality outcomes.

- A competitive element, where appropriate. Low-stress quizzes and tests that commit what they are learning to memory are important to gauge what is being learned.

- Lots of higher order, metacognitive questions (which you don't answer for them) that test out their level of learning. Every child should have the chance to ask and answer questions every lesson, whether in whole-class discussion, groups or pairs. Make them think!

However, thought is so much more than memory. We have approximately 60,000 thoughts a day. They impact on our feelings, our beliefs and our personality, and create our experience of this life. Making pupils think consciously and curiously in your lesson will help them to remember more.

> *Whatever you think about, that's what you remember. Memory is the residue of thought.*
>
> **DANIEL WILLINGHAM**[11]

- Shared visual aids and practical activities to help apply the learning, with plenty of memory techniques and learning strategies that may suit different pupils.

- A smattering of jeopardy or a moment of shock and awe. Keep them alert and engaged. Yes, do jump on a desk and read out a scary speech from history, or come into class wearing a costume or a wig. Spin a wheel of fortune to pick out a member of the class for a challenge. Anything that will enhance their memory for an important learning point is a priceless weapon in the battle against forgetting content.

Avoid cognitive overload, which can occur when you give too much information or too many tasks to learners simultaneously, resulting in them being unable to process this information.[12] Instead, chunk it into small steps. Don't move on with more information until they have absorbed each chunk of knowledge. Rephrase, review and repeat to make sure it's sinking in! (See Chapter 6 for more detail.)

Challenge, collaboration, choice and competition must be present to deliver an outstanding lesson because:

- **Challenge** is the way to ensure that expectations are high and that learners are working to *make progress* in their learning.

---

11 Willingham, *Why Don't Students Like School?*, p. 47.
12 J. Sweller, Cognitive Load During Problem Solving: Effects on Learning, *Cognitive Science* (12) (1998): 257–285.

- **Collaboration** ensures that pupils work together, independently of the teacher, to achieve brilliant outcomes.

- **Choice** engages the learners and makes them feel committed to the task.

- **Competition** encourages **commitment**. We are naturally competitive animals – winning and losing is part of life. Children need to discover that it's good to win but important to experience how to lose with grace, and learn from it. So teachers need to encourage collaborative challenges that make pupils desire to be the very best learners they can be.

New learning will always be built on prior knowledge. For example, to learn iambic pentameter you need to remember rhythm and rhyme. To do this, review, remind, and investigate how the new learning connects with what has been done before through description, questioning and discussion.

Please note, if you have an Ofsted inspection, remember that they will not:

> advocate a particular method of planning (including lesson planning), teaching or assessment; it is up to schools to determine their practices and it is up to leadership teams to justify these on their own merits rather than by referring to this handbook.[13]

Different approaches to teaching can be effective. What is appropriate will depend on the aims of the particular lesson or activity, and its place in the sequence of teaching the topic. Nevertheless, certain features must be present to ensure that the approach is delivering the desired outcomes effectively.[14] Use whatever teaching methods suit

---

13 Ofsted, *School Inspection Handbook*, p. 13.
14 Ofsted, *School Inspection Handbook*, pp. 24-25.

Research Newton's Third Law of Motion.
5 points

Research Newton's First Law of Motion.
5 points

Research Newton's Second Law of Motion.
5 points

Build a water rocket.
10 points

WATER ROCKET PROJECT

Compulsory activities.

Launch your rocket and measure the distance it travelled.
3 points

Write a detailed evaluation of the performance of your rocket.
5 points

What is PSI? Why is it important in launching a rocket?
5 points

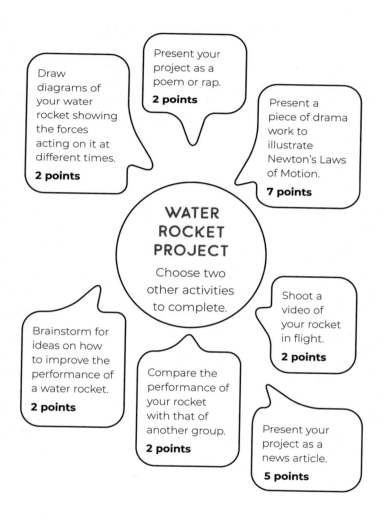

the material, so long as they meet the learners' needs and help them fulfil their potential.

GROUP WORK AND TEAMWORK

Peer pressure and support is a powerful tool for learning, so it pays to create a culture of allies. Collaborative activities can help to connect the learning with the world at home and allow the teacher to be a facilitator of learning by intervening with individuals to challenge, support or scaffold tasks. This is the very best type of differentiation, and in outstanding classroom teaching it will be evident and highly effective in meeting individual needs.

In addition, collaborative activities can be highly effective in inspiring pupils and ensuring that they learn well. However, you need to be rigorous in your monitoring of individuals' learning when group work takes place. You will know which pupils may be passengers or become disengaged easily. Intervene as necessary to make sure *all* learners benefit in group work situations. When you get the class working effectively in small groups, it helps you to improve the quality of your teaching by enabling you to:

- Use your subject knowledge to question, challenge and inspire pupils.

- Check pupils' understanding in lessons and give support to those in need.

- Give well-directed feedback which, in turn, the pupils respond to and use to make progress.

- Foster effort and a resilience to failure in your pupils and promote a love of learning and pride in their work.

- Be able to report accurately on progress to parents and others.

You can also set up group work or teamwork that develops employability or personal skills (i.e. the PLTs). But before doing this, coach pupils in the four stages of group work: forming, storming, norming and performing.[15] It is important for pupils to understand that group work can be challenging but that teamworking skills are valuable. Help them use roles within groups to maximise personal skills and work together for the best outcomes. You can build in teamwork feedback so that pupils can understand how to improve their contribution and their ability to negotiate.

Stand back and support pupils' abilities to resolve conflict in group work. There will be conflict and argument, but learning how to resolve these disputes is an important aspect of personal development.

PROJECT WORK

Collaborative projects are group challenges that involve choosing tasks around a cross-curricular or single-subject theme and completing them by negotiation. The end product will be demonstrated to the whole class and celebrated as part of the assessment.

Working together, sharing views, skills and ideas, learning to benefit from diverse thinking and enjoying success as a team – to me, these are crucial experiences that prepare our children for the world of work and develop their emotional intelligence.

Assessment for such projects can be subject- or skills-based, depending on the learning outcomes that have been set and monitored by both teachers and pupils (some examples follow). The philosophical question

---

15 See B. Tuckman, Developmental Sequence in Small Groups, *Psychological Bulletin* 63(6) (1965): 384–399.

encourages reflection and metacognitive thinking as well as higher order thinking skills. The outcomes should be presented by the group and, as far as is possible, quality control should be given to the team.

An element of competition can be added by allocating points for different tasks. The Water Rocket project on pages 86–87 is an example of this. More examples can be found at: www.jackiebeere.com.

KNOWLEDGE ORGANISERS

These are useful because they summarise all the learning for a topic on one page.[16] They can be used for mini-testing and sent home so parents can see what the learning intent is. They can be reproduced by the pupil as a mind map in their own words for deepening the understanding. Examples can be downloaded from many sources.

For a cross-curricular open-ended approach to independent learning, see the ideas in the following table for projects that add creativity, independent thinking and authentic outcomes to engage pupils.

---

16 For a discussion and examples, see J. Kirby, Knowledge Organisers, *Pragmatic Reform* [blog] (28 March 2015). Available at: https://pragmaticreformwordpress.com/2015/03/28/knowledge-organisers/.

Stimulus – involves pupil choice	PLTs focus	Philosophical question	Knowledge input	Subject links	Authentic outcome
A COMPANY Children discuss what company to form then plan their own mini enterprise/ company as a group	Enterprise skills Creative thinking Independent enquiry Effective participation	Is profit always the most important aim for a business?	Prior knowledge of any businesses Profit and loss Marketing Local products	Maths Science Literacy Oracy Art	Present your business plan to local entrepreneurs Extension Make and sell products
A TEXT (e.g. *Macbeth*)	Self-management Reflective learning Teamworking	Is ambition always a good thing?	Shakespeare's life and times Scottish history Witches and superstition	English History Geography Oracy Personal development Drama Art	A performance of part of the play to school, parents and local actors

Stimulus – involves pupil choice	PLTs focus	Philosophical question	Knowledge input	Subject links	Authentic outcome
A COUNTRY Children choose a country to study and eventually create their own	Teamworking Independent enquiry Creative thinking	What makes people feel that they belong to a country?	The physical and human geography of Britain Overview of the globe	Geography Science Sociology	Create your own country and sell it as a tourist destination at an open day
A PROBLEM Solve an important problem (e.g. global warming, traffic jams, animal extinction, overpopulation)	Creative thinking Reflective learning Independent enquiry	How do human beings solve problems?	Model a problem-solving strategy for a specific issue within: a) the school b) the local area	Geography Science Maths	Film a documentary about your problem to screen to invited relevant local dignitaries

WHAT ABOUT DIRECT INSTRUCTION?

How well does the teacher being the 'sage on the stage' work for learning?

Siegfried Engelmann studied how to improve progress for children from disadvantaged communities and his conclusion was clear.[17] Direct instruction delivers the best results. Many elements of this teaching technique are familiar and fit well with techniques that we have already discussed. Here is an outline structure of the method:

- The opening of the lesson is intended to engage pupils' attention and activate prior knowledge.

- The teacher models the concept at hand as pupils listen and observe.

- The teacher asks questions to keep pupils engaged, monitors responses, and provides praise for on-task behaviour.

- The teacher and pupils practise the concept together. The teacher signals the pupils to answer questions in unison as they review the concept.

- The teacher calls on individual pupils to ensure that they are following the lesson and have learned the concept.

- Pupils independently complete an activity which reinforces the concept learned.

- The teacher uses a tool such as a checklist or a rubric to collect data during the lesson.

---

17 S. Engelmann, *War Against the Schools' Academic Child Abuse* (Portland, OR: Halcyon House, 1992).

- After completing the lesson and looking at the collected data, the teacher decides whether or not the lesson needs to be taught again.

When teachers are given prescriptive direct instruction scripts to deliver to targeted small groups of pupils of similar ability, this method has been shown by Engelmann to be highly effective, particularly for learners who struggle. I've seen teachers who have used a similar method achieve excellent results. However, this prescriptive style may not suit all teachers and, in my opinion, does not offer opportunities for independent thinking and creativity. This method gives quality control but limits the freedom to do it our own way, follow pupils' interests and give them more ownership of the learning experience. However, if it works for your particular learners then consider direct instruction an important method to deliver content – it can be less demanding than planning more interactive lessons.

DIRECT INSTRUCTION FOR THE 21ST-CENTURY TEACHER?

What if you and members of your department planned together, as recommended by Dominic Salles?[18] Think of the time you could save if you agreed the assessment criteria and put the learning journey into one document with all the videos, PowerPoints and other resources needed. Then you all deliver from this document using similar methods, because it tells you what to teach, when and how – with homework and assessment built in. You all benefit from each other's perspective and individual skills. This could be a time- and labour-saving solution, but could feel prescriptive if it was the only game in town.

---

18 D. Salles, *The Slightly Awesome Teacher: Edu-Research Meets Common Sense* (Woodbridge: John Catt Educational, 2016).

For me, variety is the spice of life, so there will be lessons like this and others in which the pupils play a more powerful role in the learning process. In my experience, pupils may often like a predictable teacher-led lesson in which they can play a more passive role and be entertained. However, giving them more responsibility and ownership could nurture more creativity and independence – qualities that our employers are demanding. 21st-century teaching needs to do so much more than get children to remember stuff and pass exams on a hot day in July. In the UK system, a third of our children are destined to fail that test.[19]

Ask any 20-something what the most useful aspect of their schooling was in terms of preparing them for the world of work … I don't think they'll mention exams. I loved exams and I was good at them, but I know they didn't reflect my intelligence or potential. My teachers were much better at judging that.

What was the most useful thing you learned at school besides literacy and numeracy? How have you used that in work and life?

---

19 See W. Jones, A Third of Kids Are Written Off as Failures. It Doesn't Have to Be This Way, *National Numeracy* [blog] (14 March 2017). Available at: https://www.nationalnumeracy.org.uk/blog/third-kids-are-written-failures-it-doesnt-have-be-way.

STEP 6: DISH UP THE DIRT – OFTEN

DIRT = dedicated improvement and reflection time

Making time to reflect on how well your class have learned, check understanding and really respond to feedback should be a crucial part of any school day.

As mentioned previously, learning is a journey. You can remind pupils of this by frequently asking them to check their learning processes and progress. This will impact on their personal development as learners too. Ask: 'What have you learned?', 'How have you learned it?' and 'How far have you travelled towards the learning outcome?' There should be regular checkpoints in the lesson that become part of the assessment *as* learning process (more on which in Chapter 5). A mini quiz, marked by a peer, can be a useful review activity here. Ask targeted coaching questions to check learning then give some specific feedback to individuals to act on as part of your daily routine. When pupils study written feedback and actually *do* something in response, this is metacognition in action.

Marking is often the bane of our lives – something that needs to be done as part of the whole-school assessment policy. But it is valuable in that it shows the teacher's awareness of how different groups of pupils have performed and what their next steps should be. It will also give you vital information about the effectiveness of your teaching. Then again, make marking as easy for yourself as you can. Having a list of class targets that you can refer to (such as, 'Vary the beginning of your sentences' or 'Label your diagrams') is useful. Training the pupils in peer assessment and giving individuals helpful oral advice can cut down on the piles of books to mark. Mini written or spoken quizzes to review learning also allow you to cut down on marking but remain informed about their progress. One formal assessment session every few weeks and a general monitoring brief should tell you who is and who isn't making progress.

Pay attention to the most and least able, pupils with special educational needs and disabilities (SEND), girls, boys, pupils from minority ethnic backgrounds, disadvantaged children, looked-after children, etc. You need to know who these pupils are and how they are progressing. They need to know too!

When judging a school, school leaders have to evaluate the accuracy and impact of assessment by seeing if:

- Teachers use assessment for establishing pupils' starting points so that pupils achieve their potential by the end of a year or key stage.

- Assessment draws on a range of evidence of what pupils know, understand and can do across the curriculum.

- Teachers make consistent judgements about pupils' progress and attainment – for example, within a subject, across a year group and between year groups.

Make a habit of scrolling through your class books to see if your pupils have responded to your feedback by addressing your constructive criticism. If the comment 'label your diagrams' is made, it must be addressed by a pupil's response. One child called DIRT 'fix it time' in a class I observed. Reflecting on what can be improved and then actually doing it is a powerful learning experience that should take place every day.

With DIRT you can help ensure that you hit these descriptors of high-quality teaching, learning and assessment in which:

- Teachers check pupils' understanding systematically and effectively in lessons, offering effective support.

- Teachers provide pupils with incisive feedback – in line with the school's assessment policy – about what pupils can do to improve their knowledge, understanding and skills.

- The pupils use this feedback effectively.

- Pupils are eager to know how to improve their learning. They capitalise on opportunities to use feedback, written or oral, to improve.

Your feedback must help your learners build resilience so that they can deal effectively with constructive criticism and remain confident. DIRT sessions inoculate your learners against the fragile ego that can result from fake praise. They need to know exactly what they have done right and how to improve.

Resilience is a crucial habit to develop in our classrooms. Your DIRT session must remind learners who say 'I can't do this' that the sentence ends in 'yet'.[20]

REVIEWING, REFLECTING AND REDRAFTING

This is the quality control moment when pupils work on their own or together to improve their work. When pupils know what the success criteria are, they are better able to

---

20 C. Dweck, The Power of Yet [video], *TEDxNorrköping* (12 September 2014). Available at: https://www.youtube.com/watch?v=J-swZaKN2lc.

gauge their progress. But they need to focus on the quality of the work produced too. A checklist that relates to success criteria is helpful here. You could enable pupils to begin to self- or peer-assess the work they produce to encourage independence.

Working to redraft, redraft again, improve and amend against success criteria – and acting on constructive criticism – is a vital part of the learning journey. It also gives the pupils more control over – and responsibility for – the outcomes. Additionally, it prevents marking from being a mysterious process that only goes on in the teacher's head.

High-quality self-assessment and peer assessment gives learners the ability to discuss and develop their own progress. Ensure they have a copy of the success criteria so they can build accurate assessments. Train your pupils to be expert critics of each other's work by being 'kind, specific and helpful', as recommended by inspirational teacher Ron Berger.[21] This is superb training in giving and receiving objective feedback, which is an attribute that remains a lifelong challenge for all of us.

---

21 Berger, *An Ethic of Excellence*, p. 93.

STEP 7: REMEMBER THE FINAL PLENARY/REVIEW

THE MOMENT OF TRUTH: HOW FAR DID WE GET TOWARDS OUR OBJECTIVES?

At the end of the lesson a memorable plenary will sum up the learning outcomes and reinforce the learning. If all pupils haven't made progress, don't be afraid to acknowledge it. Use this as feedback and decide what your next steps will be to ensure they have *all* learned what they need to.

Deep learning means reviewing and refreshing knowledge and applying it to new contexts. Test out their understanding by giving them problems to solve using what they have learned so far. For example, if you are teaching about how gases behave, get them to blow up a balloon at home and put it in the freezer – then, next lesson, explain why it shrinks.

Help pupils to develop a language that they can use to talk about their learning and the progress they have made – and, even more importantly, *how* they learned. Give them top tips on how to remember important information (see Chapter 7) whenever you are teaching them. Get your pupils to find ways to remember things that work especially well for them.

Useful plenary techniques include:

- Pupils delivering a timed one-minute pitch, recalling the key points of the lesson to their partner.

- Having a huge learning progress arrow on the wall. Pupils pin their names to it to show how far they have progressed towards the learning outcome. They need to explain exactly what they have learned to progress to this place.

- Using sticky notes to allow pupils to record three things they have learned – these can be placed on the door on the way out or shared in groups and ranked by importance.

- Using mini whiteboards and pens to write down and show key points from the lesson.

- Holding up fingers to indicate learning progress – 5 fingers means 'I really get it', 4 means 'I mostly get it', 3 means 'I get some of it' and so on.

- A pupil sitting in a hotseat and making three points in character as an expert. They hand on to another pupil who makes two points, then one.

- Pupils writing down the key learning points from the lesson on pieces of paper, which they then fold up and put in a bag or box. You, or they, open it up next lesson and share the comments.

- Summarising the key learning in a headline. It is useful to have some mocked-up newspapers with blank headlines to hand.

- Speed dating around the room sharing what you have learned with five different people in 30 seconds. Pupils form groups to discuss and agree on the most important summary points. Then choose one person from each group to share the summary in one minute.

Always finish on time so you don't miss out the final plenary, which will allow you to draw important conclusions about the learning. It provides vital information for planning your next lesson.

KNOW YOUR IMPACT! THE FINAL PLENARY

Cut short other activities if necessary, but make sure you have this chance to assess the progress in learning because you need to know that pupils have made, and are able to demonstrate, it. This is a moment of metacognition too – what really worked for you this lesson? Where insufficient progress has been made, you need to be clear about what action you will take to address this next lesson. One of the most common criticisms of teachers made by inspectors is that they don't use assessment outcomes to inform future planning. These tips for the final plenary can help you avoid this:

LEAD LEARNER

Try briefing one of your pupils to be the lead learner, who provides a summary of 'what we have learned so far'. Check with the others to see if they have missed anything – get the rest of the class to add to their summary or fill in any gaps. (Also see the leadership roles in Appendix 1.)

TRAFFIC LIGHTS

Use a traffic light system – green for 'I got it', amber for 'nearly there' and red for 'confused'. If pupils have these cards on their desks, they can be used throughout the lesson to show how they are feeling. They then put the appropriate card in a box as they leave. This will give you an indication of how much you have to do to secure the learning next lesson.

ELEVATOR PITCH

You have one minute to sum up your learning in your own words to your partner. Imagine you get in a lift (or elevator to use this American expression) which takes one minute to reach the top floor, and you have to complete your speech before the doors open. It should take two minutes for pairs to deliver their pitches to each other. Use a bell to start and stop the lift! Then pick out one or two pupils to share theirs with the class.

MINI WHITEBOARDS

Mini whiteboards are still such a handy and popular way to check on everyone's learning. Give pupils a couple of quiz questions and get them to write down the answers and hold it up so you can see if they are getting it.

MIRROR MOMENTS

Plenaries can take place throughout the lesson. Take a moment for a mini plenary at any time in the session to gather evidence about progress and to discuss memory strategies. It's a time for pause and reflection – a mirror moment when you assess how the pupils, and you, are really doing. The message here is to take a moment for honest reflection so you know what to do next. These moments are an important part of an outstanding lesson.

PUT IT IN YOUR RUCKSACK

Occasionally, you could recap the learning by asking the pupils what they would put in their learning rucksack, treasure chest or first-aid box. Get them to write down two or three learning points which they found useful to put away for safekeeping and help them in their future learning journey. If they have any 'learning treasure' – for example, new skills which they can use again and again or light-bulb learning moments – they would go into the treasure chest for future use. Encourage metacognition to reflect on what thinking habits and learning strategies really helped this lesson and put them in the treasure chest too. Also ask if they have anything which they might put in the first-aid box – any questions or problems that they need help solving. Some teachers actually have a rucksack, a treasure chest and a first-aid box on the front desk for pupils to put their notes into.

Finish the plenary by setting the scene for the next exciting learning experience that will build on the lesson. When they come in next time, put a picture of the rucksack up and ask them to fill it with items from last lesson.

Our learners spend much of their time learning effectively at home – setting up their mobile phones, using social media and playing computer games. Make sure you link learning at school to learning at home – and cash in on their expertise!

HOMEWORK

Setting exciting challenges to complete at home that relate to work in the classroom is an important part of planning your lesson. Flipped learning means you could ask pupils to learn important content for them to use the following day. It would be quite motivational if they had to learn about, say, Stone-Age man or a French village in order to create a documentary programme in a group the next day.

Homework or extended learning can also be related to their own community or their own interests. For example, one primary school recently completed a project on local heroes, and they were tasked to look at the history of the shoe-making business in their hometown. Another example is learning the script of a Shakespeare play for a group performance the next day. If homework is set, it must be perceived as meaningful and useful for consolidating or applying learning. (See Appendix 3 for more ideas about how to get learners to stretch themselves at home.)

Please note: There is no expected prescriptive structure to a lesson, but you need to be clear about what you are teaching and how you will measure your impact.

Learn what works and teach with passion.

SUMMARY

Great teachers make sure ...

Their pupils are less often:	Their pupils more often:	Their pupils' work shows that:	Their classroom has:
Told what to do.	Help decide what to aim for and how to go about it.	Teacher feedback notes strengths and gives specific advice for improvement.	Walls used for learning, with displays of key words and exemplars.
Left not knowing an answer.	Are shown exemplars and models of best work.	The feedback is understood and acted on by the pupil.	Some interactive displays, such as a suggestions wall with ideas for future lessons.
Set objectives they don't understand or care about.	Are engaged with the objectives and set their own success criteria.	They are interactive with their work.	Quality work displayed, accurate in terms of spelling and presentation.
Having to wait for feedback.	Use the success criteria to reflect on and assess their work and progress.	There is improvement over time and progress can be seen.	
Passive or coasting.			
Formally assessed by an adult, scheme or authority.			

Assessed at the end of their work when it is too late to improve it.	Use success criteria to sum up what they have learned and to seek feedback.	Any targets are understood.	Displays which promote the good habits of great learners, such as resilience, empathy, using feedback, risk-taking, listening, collaborating and teamwork.
Left little or no time to respond to feedback.	Know how to improve learning and memory.	Care is taken with presentation.	Displays that encourage reflection on success criteria and the learning journey.
Given levels or grades as a record of their progress and achievement.	Have more feedback during their work than at the end, and *do* something about it.	Tasks are completed accurately.	A wall used once a term to collect feedback from pupils, such as a Keep, Change, Grow display.
Peer-assessed inaccurately.	Have time to reflect and act on the feedback given.	There is evidence of correction and practice.	
Finding it hard to remember what they have been taught.	Know that critical feedback will help them improve.	They have learned how to use knowledge in different contexts.	
	Have support that helps them develop their own strategies and thinking skills.		

Great teachers make sure ...			
Their pupils are less often:	**Their pupils more often:**	**Their pupils' work shows that:**	**Their classroom has:**
	Make connections to previous learning.		
	Are developing a growth mindset and the habits of great learners.		
	Peer- and self-assess accurately and habitually.		
	Are very ambitious and aspirational in their learning.		

CHAPTER 4

MANAGING THE CLASSROOM – PREPARE TO BE PRESENT AND TAKE CONTROL

You – like all teachers – will have had lessons in which it all goes wrong, children misbehave, and you think you are a rubbish teacher. Don't beat yourself up about it – the good news is that the children are unlikely to have attached the same importance to it. Each lesson is a chance to get it right – or better than ever before.

Sometimes it's hard to be the best that we can be at the precise moment it is needed. This chapter aims to help you understand how to perform at your best when you need to. It also emphasises the vital role of relationships in the classroom.

PREPARING FOR THE OBSERVER IN YOUR CLASSROOM: THE MIND–BODY CONNECTION

Visualise success. We all run through future challenging scenarios in our heads – often predicting the worst outcomes – so make sure you deliberately envisage success.

Mentally rehearse your lesson before you get there. This will ensure that your unconscious knows clearly how to behave without you having to think too much about it. Like a car in cruise control, you'll be able to trust your unconscious mind to deliver results. This is an important part of your preparation. When you do your mental rehearsal, make sure that you are saying the phrases shown on pages 117–118.

Imagine that your lesson is planned and you have your resources ready – including water to drink. See yourself with positive body language – standing tall, head up, in control of the class but relaxed and smiling. Breathe deeply, slowly and regularly. Use the mantras in this book to trigger your memory of what works well. Imagine meeting and greeting the pupils. Look as if you are really enjoying it and hear your voice – strong, loud and authoritative, full of warmth and sincerity. Calm the class, praise them, explain the objectives and tasks. Move around the classroom with confidence. Hover around the pupils who may need extra focus and give them positive attention when they are on task. Ask questions about their learning, make them think hard. See their smiling, focused faces giving you their full attention. Take a moment to breathe and assess how well the lesson is going. Always make eye contact on a one-to-one level.

Regularly sweep the room to ensure you know *everything* that is going on – both in front of you and behind your back. This is very important, especially when you have an official observer. Believe that you have eyes in the back of your head in every lesson. (Nothing is more powerful for effective behaviour management than giving the message that you know exactly what is happening in one corner of the room, even when you are helping pupils in the opposite corner.) With pupils who are working collaboratively and in teams, see yourself moving around and supporting their learning but keeping half your attention on the whole classroom to ensure a positive working atmosphere. When the rehearsal is over, feel that you are now prepared, confident and ready for the lesson.

'This is what I was born for' – make this your mantra for the observation!

Being present in the classroom means that you are 'in the moment' and all your energy and focus is concentrated. Our attention can easily be hijacked by visitors, distracting behaviour from certain individuals, activity outside the room, our own problems, nervousness about the situation and so on.

Ruthlessly attend to the teaching you are delivering and allow nothing to divert you from this. We have all experienced that moment when we become conscious of the sound of our own voice while speaking, which can lead to anxiety sabotaging our performance. Just stay in the moment, focus your conscious attention on what you are saying and on the pupils in your classroom. Don't allow your mind to wander. This way, you will perform at your best and maintain the authenticity that is essential for the lesson to work well.

PRACTISE WHAT YOU PREACH

Great teachers have a philosophy that says, 'Every mistake is a learning experience.' Make sure that you endorse this philosophy in your own working life. You will have bad lessons – lessons that go horribly wrong and make you feel like you should give up. If you are unlucky, these experiences may happen when someone is observing. If you put into practice the philosophy of learning from your mistakes, and make this a professional habit, then you will always be able to adapt when a lesson goes wrong.

First, recognise when the lesson is going, or has gone, wrong and try something different. Second, admit your mistakes – especially to the pupils. Get feedback from them as to why it didn't work and learn from this. Third, appreciate that you can't know everything – sometimes they will know more than you (especially about social media!). Exploit this and get them to share their expertise. Be confident that being a teacher doesn't mean you have to know everything – but you do know your subject and how to help kids learn. One of the most impressive aspects of the best lessons is seeing pupils take over and do some of the teaching. Teaching each other is one of the best ways in which pupils deepen their own learning, so do it often.

Finally, if the lesson takes an unexpected turn – but this new direction serves to extend their learning – don't simply stick to your plan. Explain that this is a great development and that you are going to deviate from your lesson plan to make the most of this new opportunity for learning. For example, if a pupil has a story that relates to the lesson, let them tell it, then ask, 'What can we learn from this that fits with our learning outcome?' However, make sure this isn't just a hobbyhorse of yours or of interest to only a small group of pupils.

BEHAVIOUR MANAGEMENT

Welcome the pupils into your classroom by name, set clear boundaries for behaviour that you consistently enforce and demonstrate an infectious enthusiasm for learning.

Simples, eh?

Unfortunately, we know it can often be harder than this! Working hard on building consistent classroom relationships is the key to managing behaviour. Respect for each other and respect for the teacher should be habitual behaviours that characterise your classroom. If the lesson is interesting and expectations are high, behaviour management will not usually be a problem.

Peer pressure can be a huge lever for learning. Make it work for you by nurturing an atmosphere in which the pupils know that the more they support each other's learning, the more they will make outstanding progress themselves. When pupils are speaking or answering, everyone in the classroom should want to help them make progress. There must be zero tolerance of mockery and putdowns and massive praise for pupils who can offer constructive criticism and feedback, given with love. This is what I mean by unconditional support: when it becomes a habit, it takes place with or without the teacher in the classroom. A classroom of allies will support everyone to make more progress.

OFSTED ALERT: WHAT AN OBSERVER IS LOOKING FOR

Pupils behave with consistently high levels of respect for others. They play a highly positive role in creating a school environment in which commonalities are identified and celebrated, difference is valued and nurtured, and bullying, harassment and violence are never tolerated.

Pupils consistently have highly positive attitudes and commitment to their education. They are highly

> *motivated and persistent in the face of difficulties. Pupils make a highly positive, tangible contribution to the life of the school and/or the wider community. Pupils actively support the well-being of other pupils.*
>
> *Pupils behave consistently well, demonstrating high levels of self-control and consistently positive attitudes to their education. If pupils struggle with this, the school takes intelligent, fair and highly effective action to support them to succeed in their education.*[1]

If your teaching is being judged, enlist the support of your pupils – be open about what will happen when an observer speaks to them and asks them about their learning. Encourage them to be open and honest and answer in as much detail as possible. Be clear about how important they are to this process. Often teachers say, 'This is not about you being inspected, it's about me – so don't worry.' This is just not true – and the pupils know it. Their books will be checked, they will be asked questions and listened to. How they respond will be an important part of the judgement, so explain why all this happens and describe how they can talk about their learning and progress. Remind them to use the language for learning that you have developed with them.

If any pupils behave badly, address the behaviour immediately and follow through with any sanctions. Follow the school's behaviour policy (not your own version) rigorously and consistently in *all* your lessons and do the same if you are observed. It will be clear if this is your 'typical' response to bad behaviour.

---

1   Ofsted, *School Inspection Handbook*, p. 56.

Make sure you have specific strategies to deal with those more challenging individuals in your class to ensure that, in your lesson, they want to learn, and that they know for sure that you will deal with them consistently and rigorously. Tell them 'I will never give up on you' frequently – and mean it!

LOVE YOUR PUPILS

It is a basic tenet of neuroscience that learning is an emotional experience. Nothing is more important than you and the aura that you project in the classroom. This includes your relationship with the pupils and your belief in yourself as a great teacher. As Independent Thinking Associate Andrew Curran says in the introduction to *The Little Book of Big Stuff About the Brain*:

> *The most surprising message for me from looking through billions of dollars of research is that the most important thing you can do for yourself and for others is to love yourself and others for who they are, because by doing that you maximise the brain's ability to learn and unlearn.*[2]

Loving your pupils can require high-quality acting and performing skills! But, as many teachers have discovered, such performances can become a reality. You can learn to love them – even the 'hardcore' pupils: the ones who seem determined to make you dislike them by challenging your authority and who refuse to participate in learning activities that have taken hours of careful thought and planning. Many of us have surprised ourselves by using that tried and tested method of 'pretending' that our least favourite class is, in fact, the class we most enjoy teaching.

---

2   Curran, *The Little Book of Big Stuff About the Brain*, p. 1.

How do you do this? Simple! Arrive early, instead of as late as possible. Wait at the door with a smile and a personal greeting, especially for the most challenging individuals. Set the highest expectations of behaviour and learning in your opening communications and be consistent in sticking to them in every lesson and with every pupil. Children love strict teachers who they can respect and who respect and value them. The most unlovable pupils are the ones most in need of love from their teacher. Deliberately make every child (especially the invisible) feel that they are secretly your favourite.

BUILD RAPPORT

Communication skills are the most crucial skills that a teacher needs to ensure the best outcomes in lessons – but it is so easy to get it wrong. Rapport exists when you have connected with your audience and they want to be there listening. You know you have it when people look, smile and respond to you. When you don't have rapport, you can be as knowledgeable and clever as you like, but no one will be listening.

You get rapport through using an appropriate register and body language. Make it too formal and the pupils will turn off. Instead, use open, confident body language, good volume and intonation that sounds enthusiastic – even passionate – about your subject. Connect with their state of mind, calibrate, adapt and tune in to the mood of the classroom. Connect with their world by understanding it. Music, sport, television, computer games – whatever it takes – make sure you know what matters to them and try to use it in your teaching. Your job is to create a 'can do' and 'will do' philosophy and to nurture an atmosphere in which making mistakes is accepted as an integral part of learning. Be consistent in this. *Every* lesson!

BE A ROLE MODEL FOR COMMUNICATION SKILLS

You must be articulate and literate if you are a teacher or TA. We all sometimes make mistakes with spelling and grammar. If you are unsure, admit it, check it and correct it. Be a role model for standard English because this is the gift that will support your 'disadvantaged' children to aspire to the careers they want, and to challenge the social class barriers. Set relentlessly high standards of literacy for yourself and others.

The language you use develops mindsets – yours and theirs. Have a look at these simple examples of how we can communicate with our pupils to set the mood for learning and create positive mindsets:

'Good morning! How is my favourite class today?'

'Anything exciting happen at the weekend?'

'I'm really looking forward to teaching you this bit as you're going to love it.'

'I was really impressed with what some of you did for homework. It's some of the best work I've ever seen.'

'Some of you have found it hard but that's good because we are going to learn why, sort it out and get you making great progress.'

'We'll find a way to help you learn this.'

'You are the best class I teach.'

'I love the way you work together so well.'

'You've come up with the most amazing ideas.'

'You've made my day with the work you've produced.'

'I need you to listen and work hard because I know you can do it.'

'When you're at football practice, you're so determined. Let's see if you can find some of that motivation and apply it here for me.'

'The way this class supports each other in their learning is outstanding and makes me very proud.'

'No matter what happens I will never give up on you because I know you can be a great learner.'

'Well done for working so hard on that. Tell me what you've learned so far and what else you would like to learn.'

'Brilliant. That work you are doing shows just how hard you're working. What do you need to do to progress further?'

'You're thinking really hard about what you have to do, and you'll really make great progress if you carry on like this.'

'You've redrafted this so many times and that's exactly what you need to do to produce an outstanding piece of writing. Superb effort!'

'You didn't get that right *yet*, but you kept trying and learned from your mistakes – that makes you a brilliant learner.'

> *Parents think that they can hand children permanent confidence – like a gift – by praising their brains and talent. It doesn't work, and in fact has the opposite effect. It makes children doubt themselves as soon as anything is hard, or anything goes wrong. If parents want to give their children a gift, the best thing they can do is teach their children to love challenges, be intrigued by mistakes, enjoy effort, and keep on learning.*
>
> **CAROL DWECK**[3]

Dweck's research shows us that if we want to develop growth mindsets, it's not enough to tell pupils just to work harder or that they should be getting top marks. You need to help them develop strategies for learning and thinking that work for their individual needs and praise their efforts in doing this more than you praise the outcome. Praise them when they are making progress through persistence, determination and high-quality work.

Alternatively, we can set them up to fail. Here's what not to say (though we have all been tempted to utter words like these at times!):

'You lot never know how to behave.'

'Let's not have another lesson where we waste your time and mine.'

'We have to get through this bit for the exam, even though it's hard and boring.'

'I can't believe how many of you just haven't made the effort for homework. You'll never learn anything unless you make more effort.'

3   Dweck, *Mindset*, p. 176.

'You're really struggling with this, so you need to concentrate harder.'

'You're the worst class in Year 8 because you just don't listen.'

'If you don't get on with your work, you're wasting my time, so I'll waste your time in break.'

'I don't enjoy this any more than you do.'

'I am so disappointed by the way you are behaving.'

'What would your parents say if they saw how you are behaving?'

Catching them being good and praising that behaviour will always work better than generalisations and negative predictions.

Also, praising the outcome alone can make pupils think that this is the most important and that the effort, skills and strategies they used to achieve it are less so. Some pupils who continually get praised for excellent results may become reluctant to try harder challenges if they think that they won't succeed – and thus learn to limit their learning. So, don't say:

'Brilliant, 10/10 – a fantastic result. I want to see this every time.'

'This is excellent work – with your ability, I expect nothing less.'

'At last, a pass grade – this is more worthwhile!'

Dweck's research also shows that when we praise effort when it is not warranted, it actually undermines the recipient's respect and confidence in us. Especially don't say, 'That's brilliant!' – when it plainly isn't.

This is important information for parents too, so you might want to share with them the useful checklist that follows.

GROWTH MINDSET DOS AND DON'TS

Sometimes we don't realise how words that we think encourage and praise can actually undermine a pupil's potential, stopping them becoming the best learner they can be. Every word or action sends a message.

Are you sending messages that support them to grow as resilient learners? Consider this:

Do	Do say	Don't	Don't say
Praise effort as well as outcome. Avoid praising intelligence.	*I'm very impressed by how hard you are trying and how much you are learning.*	Praise their intelligence and talents – as if they are fixed.	*You must get 10/10 – it's the only result that matters because you are so clever.*

Do	Do say	Don't	Don't say
Give lots of feedback about how they have done and what they could do next – without criticising and making personal judgements.	*You've written such an exciting story – how about redrafting it and checking some of the spellings that I have underlined?*	Judge their outcomes – either good or bad – without giving points for improvement. Mix up judgement of outcomes with that of personal qualities.	*You're so talented, I expected more from you.* *This is full of mistakes. You can do better!*
Focus on what they are learning and developing and celebrate that.	*You've really tried hard with those problems – how did you work them out?*	Make them feel like the only thing that matters is their grades.	*You need to get good results if you're ever going to be successful.*
Help them realise that mistakes are a part of learning and that you only learn by sticking at it until you can make progress.	*Did you find that text hard with all that difficult vocabulary? Just think how much you are learning if you get through it all.*	Get irritated if they can't do it – or imply that you think they are useless or 'thick'.	*There's no way you will be able to read that – it's much too difficult.*

Do	Do say	Don't	Don't say
Model a growth mindset yourself by sometimes getting it wrong and showing how you learn from mistakes.	*Who can help me with this technology/ maths/ spelling problem as I'm struggling and I want to get it right?*	Demonstrate that you are stuck in your ways and nervous about learning new things.	*I don't do technology/ maths/ spelling – never have been able to ...*
Praise them for specific achieve-ments and for their persistence.	*I'm impressed with how you have found a new way to understand algebra. You stuck at it and didn't give up until you found a way.*	Only praise them when they get it *all* right. They should be tackling work that is hard enough to get some things wrong.	*I want to see an A* from you every time.*
Help them fix it when they make mistakes. Make sure they are willing to challenge themselves, not opt for guaranteed success.	*Hey! You got it wrong – that's good because it shows you can keep learning.*	Make fixed judgements about their ability and compare them with others.	*You should be coming top of the class with your ability.*

Do	Do say	Don't	Don't say
Talk to them about the learning process and journey.	*What have you learned today that has really pushed your comfort zone?*	Let them think that you can learn and make progress without the pain of hard work!	*All that matters is the exam grade you get, I don't care how you get there.*
Help them choose challenging tasks that stretch them, even if they might not get everything right.	*Isn't it exciting when you're working really hard on something and eventually you get it!*	Allow them to just do the things they know that they are good at.	*Stick with what you know – at least you will get a good mark.*

Don't get mad, get curious.

CHAPTER 5

ASSESSMENT *IS* LEARNING

The assessment evolution:

What was — **Assessment *of* learning**
(Marking to gauge knowledge and understanding.)

became — **Assessment *for* learning**
(Assessment that supports progress.)

then — **Assessment *as* learning**
(Assessment that is part of the learning process.)

but could now be: — **Assessment *is* learning**
(Assessment process is learning in itself as a continuous internal and external review of progress.)

> *Assessment for learning is the process of seeking and interpreting evidence for use by pupils and their teachers, to decide where the pupils are in their learning, where they need to go and how best to get there.*
>
> **PATRICIA BROADFOOT ET AL.**[1]

---

1   P. Broadfoot, R. Daugherty, J. Gardner, W. Harlen, M. James and G. Stobart, Assessment for Learning: 10 Principles. Research-Based Principles to Guide Classroom Practice (Assessment Reform Group, 2002). Available at: https://www.researchgate.net/publication/271849158_Assessment_for_Learning_10_Principles_Research-based_principles_to_guide_classroom_practice_Assessment_for_Learning.

Assessment is such an important part of the process of learning, and of making progress in learning, that it deserves a chapter in its own right. The argument put forward by Dylan Wiliam and Paul Black in *Inside the Black Box* – that formative assessment is an essential component of classroom work and can raise pupil achievement – has been won.[2] Assessment for learning policy and practice has been driving school improvement strategies in the years since that book was published because it works.

Your pupils should be able to discuss their learning and what they need to do to improve. The work they produce will show marking and targets for improvement and it should be evident from this that your pupils respond to feedback and make progress over time. Since feedback has been recognised as a crucial aspect of effective teaching, a variety of methods have become popular. Live marking as described by Ross Morrison McGill can be done in the classroom verbally, with the aid of a coloured pen.[3] It works by zooming in on one part of a page of work and giving intense, detailed feedback to elicit an immediate pupil response, which, additionally, is a powerful teacher–pupil interaction. When time is short, keep it brief and skim their work, picking out useful tips – I call this drive-by marking. It helps you to keep a close eye on how they are doing, and your presence mooching around the desks makes pupils feel that you care.

One helpful description of an assessment-centred classroom is as follows:

> *In assessment-centred classrooms, assessment is both formative and summative and becomes a tool to aid learning: pupils monitor their progress over time and with*

2   D. Wiliam and P. Black, *Inside the Black Box: Raising Standards Through Classroom Assessment* (London: GL Assessment, 2006).

3   R. Morrison McGill, *Mark. Plan. Teach.* (London: Bloomsbury Education, 2017).

their teachers identify the next steps needed to improve. Techniques such as open questioning, sharing learning objectives and focused marking have a powerful effect on students' ability to take an active role in their learning. There is always sufficient time left for reflection by students. Whether individually or in pairs, students are given the opportunity to review what they have learned and how they have learned it. They evaluate themselves and one another in a way that contributes to understanding. Students know their levels of achievement and make progress towards their next goal.

DAVID HARGREAVES[4]

Verbal feedback stamps can provide evidence that teachers are talking to pupils. These are perhaps useful as a reminder, but good teachers give verbal advice, coaching and feedback continually throughout lessons, and we shouldn't formalise a natural interaction – in my opinion. Weave around the classroom, pen in hand, zooming in on work to give useful guidance, underlining, highlighting and using every available strategy to make the pupils self-reflect and correct.

This type of teaching encourages independent learning as it gives pupils the tools for monitoring their own progress. It also links to the PLTs framework (which, as I've mentioned, I still see as useful despite it no longer being the policy du jour) as it involves the development of reflective learning, self-management and independent enquiry, and it fits perfectly with the personal development aspect of school inspection.[5] A mix of classroom intervention, periodic assessment, targets to fit in with whole-school policy, and self- and peer-marking must provide feedback

---

4 D. Hargreaves (chair), *About Learning: Report of the Learning Working Group* (London: Demos, 2005), p. 17.

5 See Ofsted, *School Inspection Handbook*, pp. 58-64.

about progress but *not* give the teacher an unreasonable workload.

Compare your own practice against the following advice about assessment *as* learning.

SELF-ASSESSMENT

Good teachers need to encourage the habit of self-assessment against the learning objectives and success criteria until it becomes routine. As Ross Morrison McGill emphasises in *Mark. Plan. Teach.*, the purpose of assessment, feedback and marking is to help pupils value hard work and the quality of the work that they produce.[6] Self-assessment, as a regular activity, accentuates this responsibility and counteracts the perception that it is the teacher's job to judge work and effort. The assessment objectives for your subject may help pupils to self-assess accurately but they will probably need translating into simple categories. Mini quizzes, low-stakes tests and timed recall games are all good techniques to help them learn how to build and test their memory skills. Press the pause button and let them see how much they have retained. 'How are we doing?' and 'How do you know?' are important questions for the teacher or TA who wants to be a change agent.

---

6   Morrison McGill, *Mark. Plan. Teach.*

PEER ASSESSMENT

Opportunities for peer assessment are vital in a great lesson. You need to have built up the skills to help your pupils to do it well over time, which will require a culture of trust and respect. This, in turn, provides excellent evidence of the quality of your teaching. To nurture great peer assessment, you need to show pupils how important they are to each other's learning. Use the following five-point plan:

1 Teach pupils that 'I can learn more by helping others learn', and that when they assess each other's work through high-quality peer critique, it improves their own performance. After all, having played the role of assessor, they know what is required to impress.

2 Create a culture of unconditional support of each other's learning. Reinforce an atmosphere in which the pupils listen to each other, care about each other making good progress and appreciate constructive criticism. Kind, specific, helpful advice from a peer is priceless.

3 Have zero tolerance of disrespect towards the effort of others. This must apply when pupils are marking each other's work and when they are listening to each other's presentations.

4 Make sure they know and understand the success criteria when assessing each other's work. They can then write targets for each other as they mark. This will help them to understand how to improve their own work too.

5 Encourage them to discover and share useful memory strategies and learning skills. Reward high-quality peer assessment as much as you can.

QUESTIONING – THE ESSENTIAL TEACHING TOOL FOR ASSESSMENT *AS* LEARNING IN THE CLASSROOM

The teacher's questions don't just make pupils think, they also measure understanding – or lack of it. They are an essential tool of the trade, so include them in your planning. Doug Lemov describes using 'cold calls' – whereby pupils don't know if you will call on them to answer – and 'wait time' – whereby you always provide time to think or discuss with a partner before the answer is requested.[7] The bonus is that all the pupils will be busy thinking, in case you follow up with a question to test their understanding. Use open questions that encourage analysis, synthesis and evaluation at critical learning moments to elicit thinking and develop learning. You can do this when pupils are working on an individual basis or during class discussion.

Some more tried and trusted strategies to help with successful questioning follow. Don't be afraid to adapt and make them work in your own way.

- **Vary your no-hands-up policy.** If no one can put their hand up, they all have to think about the question – especially when you then pick a name from a hat and expect an answer.

- **Thinking time: pair and share.** Set questions that the pupils can think about in pairs and get them to come up with several possible answers to share with the rest of the class.

---

7   D. Lemov, *Teach Like a Champion 2.0: 62 Techniques That Put Students on the Path to College* (San Francisco, CA: Jossey-Bass, 2015).

- **Use connectives to extend thinking.** Ask them to use connectives such as 'but', 'therefore', 'however' and 'alternatively' like batons to extend answers. After one pupil answers, the next one must take over and add to it using their chosen connective.

- **Reflect and review.** Use metacognition to reflect on *what* has been learned and *how* it has been learned. As well as identifying what supported the learning (resources, research, friends, trying a different method, etc.), reflect on the mistakes made and the obstacles that got in the way (distractions, limiting beliefs, lack of understanding or prior knowledge, skill deficit, etc.).

- **Question the learning.** Ask the pupils to make up a set of questions about what they have learned and what questions they need to ask for the next stage of their progress. This will require demonstrating an understanding of what they have learned and where they are now.

- **Pose, pause, pounce, bounce.** This is a simple and effective idea, which was devised by Pam Fearnley at Pupils First UK Ltd.[8] Questions should be posed by the teacher or other pupils, and followed by a pause to allow everyone to think or discuss possible answers. One pupil is then pounced on for their answer, and their answer is bounced to a different pupil with another question – for example, 'Do you agree with that answer?' and then to another pupil: 'How can we find out if that is right?' The aim is to involve as many pupils as possible in the thinking process.

---

8   Thank you to Pam Fearnley of Pupils First UK (wwwqhist.com), who can be contacted at: pamb566@btinternet.com.

Socratic questioning is at the heart of critical thinking. Using these types of open questions in the classroom, and for homework, will help you to deepen pupils' understanding and embed knowledge:

QUESTIONS FOR CLARIFICATION

- Why do you say that?
- How does this relate to our discussion?
- Are you going to include your working out in your equations?

QUESTIONS THAT PROBE ASSUMPTIONS

- What else could be causing this?
- How can you find out if that is true?
- Why are you using the same source to get your evidence as last time?

QUESTIONS THAT PROBE REASONS AND EVIDENCE

- What would be an example?
- What is this similar to?
- Why do you think X causes Y to happen?
- Do you think that exercise will always make you fit?

QUESTIONS ABOUT VIEWPOINTS AND PERSPECTIVES

- What would be an alternative?
- What is another way to look at it?

- Would you explain why it is necessary and who benefits?

- What are the strengths and weaknesses of X?

- How are X and Y similar?

- How could we prevent traffic jams, and would this be good for everyone?

QUESTIONS THAT PROBE IMPLICATIONS AND CONSEQUENCES

- What could happen now?

- What generalisations can you make?

- What are the consequences of that assumption?

- What are you implying?

- How does X affect Y?

- How does X connect with what we learned before?

- What would happen if you didn't come to school?

QUESTIONS ABOUT THE QUESTION

- What was the point of that question?

- Why do you think I asked that question?

- How does X apply to everyday life?

- Why do you need to learn this?

These questions deepen knowledge and challenge pupils, encouraging flexible thinking and an open mind. The very best teachers know the level of progress that each answer represents.

QUESTIONING THAT PROMOTES AND PROBES THINKING

Teacher: What makes you think that photosynthesis is vital for our planet … Jake?

Jake: Because nothing could live without it.

Teacher: Why would nothing live?

Jake: Well, the process makes life possible.

Teacher: How does photosynthesis make life possible? Help him out … Kami.

Kami: Is it because plants take in carbon dioxide and water and produce oxygen?

Teacher: How does that help us?

Kami: Plants use the CO_2 and H_2O to make sugars, using energy from the sun to do it. They can then combine the sugars with minerals from the ground to make all the chemicals that plants, and the animals that eat them, need to live and grow. The oxygen is produced as a by-product of photosynthesis but is useful for plant and animal respiration.

Teacher: Excellent, Kami! Now can you help show Jake how this works using a diagram?

ASSESSMENT FOR LEARNING IN THE CLASSROOM: WHAT IS THE DIFFERENCE BETWEEN GOOD AND OUTSTANDING?

Good (the pupils do all of this):

- All pupils know what they are learning and why.

- Pupils know the success criteria and can self-assess their work against them.

- Pupils learn openly from each other frequently.

- Pupils ask reflective questions of their own and others' work.

- Pupils can constructively criticise each other to support learning.

- All pupils make good progress with developing independence.

Outstanding (the pupils do all of the above *plus* all of this):

- All pupils understand and can talk about their learning outcomes and set their own individual success criteria.

- Pupils can use subject terminology and language for learning to discuss and monitor their own progress.

- Pupils value talking for learning and consciously use it to advance their learning.

- Pupils' questions demonstrate fearless enquiry and a desire to progress.

- Pupils know exactly where they are, what they have achieved and how to make further progress.

Good (*you* do all of this):

- Plan and set challenging and clear objectives that engage *all* pupils.

- Encourage pupils to set success criteria for the learning outcomes.

- Make links to other subjects and contexts.

- Ensure that pupils know their grades of progression.

- Review progress with pupils regularly throughout the lesson.

- Use skilful questioning and resources to encourage sustained successful collaborative work.

- Are flexible and respond to learning needs – adjusting whenever appropriate to make maximum progress.

- Your marking is focused and sets clear targets that relate to learning needs and engage pupils, so they take action.

Outstanding (*you* do all of the above *plus* all of this):

- Set big goals and have very high expectations of all pupils in the lesson and over time.

- Plan progression in the PLTs and subject concepts as an integral part of the lesson.

- Constantly coach pupils in understanding how their learning is progressing and how to recognise it.

- Skilfully develop class discussion to nurture thinking and encourage independence.

- Develop the learning together with the pupils in response to the advancement made.

● Plan next steps with pupils in response to the progress made in the lesson.

● Show clear evidence that your marking impacts on pupils by helping them to make exceptional progress.

MAKE FEEDBACK WORK FOR YOU AND FOR THEM

The most important and powerful aspect of assessment *as* learning is that it is not a tick list of activities but rather it shows your (and the pupils') clear engagement with the process of learning. It involves coaching your pupils to move relentlessly forward in their knowledge, skills and understanding. It is an integral and flexible part of your teaching, your conversations with your pupils, the work in their books and their progress over time.

There has been much concern about the way in which marking impacts on teachers' workload, with policy makers agreeing that a school's assessment policy should not result in unnecessary extra work.[9] It is up to each school to work with teachers to set a policy that delivers feedback about progress to pupils and teachers, and which also helps teachers to spend their time and energy on teaching – not on wading through piles of books. Marking with a specific focus on progress a couple of times a term, and using an interactive approach during lesson time, is a popular option that can still deliver evidence of:

● Pupils' effort and success in completing their work, both in and outside lessons, so that they can progress and enjoy learning across the curriculum.

---

9   See the Department for Education guidance at: https://www.gov.uk/government/publications/feedback-and-marking-reducing-teacher-workload.

- The level of challenge and whether pupils have to grapple appropriately with content, not necessarily 'getting it right' first time.

- How well teachers' feedback – written and oral – is used by pupils to improve their knowledge, understanding and skills.

- How written and oral feedback is used to promote learning.

We have already seen how DIRT offers an important opportunity to take advantage of the individual differentiated support you can give your pupils. A little coaching about how they can respond to your feedback by taking positive action will make your marking much more effective. Take the opportunity to laser mark (by which I mean zooming in on particular pupils' books to highlight learning opportunities) during DIRT time. Scan the pupils' work and when you identify some useful advice, give it verbally or with a note. Love seeing the way your pupils have progressed, hate piles of books to mark? Make drive-by marking (see page 126) a habit in lessons.

TOP TIPS

- Plan your lessons by writing down the key questions to be answered and link these to levels of progression or exam grades.

- Wander the classroom regularly giving verbal and written feedback.

- Mark in detail according to the school policy to assess progress and set targets for improvement.

- Use mini quizzes and low-stakes testing frequently to assess the impact of your teaching and find out what to review.

- Encourage peer critique using kind, specific, helpful feedback.

- Ask coaching-style, Socratic questions that make pupils think for themselves – for example, 'What do you think will happen next if you do that?'

- Allow thinking time and paired thinking to better explore possible answers and engage more pupils.

- Use mini whiteboards or electronic devices to enable *all* pupils to attempt to answer questions.

- Welcome unexpected answers and build on them to reconstruct your lesson.

- Respond to wrong answers by showing that they are an excellent addition to our learning journey!

- Encourage pupils to pose their own questions – set this as homework.

- Always ask of yourself and the pupils: 'How will learning this be useful in your life outside school?'

CASE STUDY: A YEAR 5 LITERACY LESSON

As you walk into Sue's lesson, there is a buzz of activity, with 26 children grouped around tables working on various literacy tasks according to their current targets and individual needs.

One group, containing mainly boys, are working with the teacher using tablets, discovering various tools and apps to improve their spelling. I spoke to a mixed ability group about their learning, and they were working on what can only be described as very challenging words and phrases to extend their vocabulary. On the table were laminated quotes like, 'All thinking begins with wondering' and 'Apply past knowledge to new situations'. Pupils could explain what these statements meant and why they were relevant in each case.

Each child also had a badge. Suddenly the *Pink Panther* theme music came on for a few seconds and those with the learning spy badge were off on their mission to 'spy' on other groups' good ideas to help them with their own task. When asked if they resented someone stealing their work, the indignant reply was, 'Well, that's how we learn – from each other and by trying out new ideas.' Other badges for class leadership included ogre (peer assessor), word monster (the scribe), brain teaser (who develops flexible thinking habits) and ii, which also had a picture of two eyes (for the pupil given the job of being the work checker).

What was most impressive was the way in which these roles were acted out with conviction and understanding – as if interdependent learning was just part of what they always do. The lowest ability group, which had been working on tablets, were then tasked with teaching the others in small groups about how to use the app Word Mess to extend their skills in spelling and vocabulary.

The quality of the work in books was as high as I have seen in Year 9 English lessons, and the marking supported progress with feedback that helped pupils focus on how to improve. Some wonderful writing, completed as an 'Ogre report', was adventurous and exciting.

The pupils I spoke to were impressively articulate about their learning and about how they could improve. It was clear that they understood what progress looked like and were also encouraged to have an active engagement with their learning journey.

We paused as the teacher gathered pupils on the mat and checked out prior learning about an author's writing that had been set as homework. A line of pictures of babies showing different moods across the top of the wall was used as a continuum for assessing their starting point for the task. This was a fun way to consider how much the pupils thought they knew and was clearly used regularly. Music was then used for children to move from one table to another, swapping and growing their factual knowledge about the author and her work. Each time the music stopped, the pupils moved on and shared another new fact that then had to be explained to the next person.

One pupil then gave a PowerPoint presentation that he had put together as his homework, extending the knowledge about the author and the books she had written. He finished this with an interactive quiz for the class to check what they had learned from his session! Finally, following examples of examining and analysing the writing style, pupils attempted an extended writing task of their own.

The strengths of this lesson were evident in the way the pupils demonstrated embedded learning skills through what each child said and did in the short time I was there. They could articulate what they were doing, knew how they could improve and what strategies they could use when stuck. All ability levels were challenged and excited about their learning. On the wall was a Suggestions and Reflections board where pupils could put forward their ideas for how things could be improved in future lessons.

Looking through their books, there was clear evidence of marking which had set targets that had been responded to. An example of this was where vocabulary had been underlined in a story, and the pupil asked to look at these words and try to improve the impact on the reader. The pupil had replaced the words with very complex adjectives and adverbs, and when questioned he could tell me what they meant and why he had chosen them.

Some comments from pupils about their teacher were: 'She tells us exactly what we need to improve on', 'She makes us practice so that we remember and never give up', 'It's always fun and she is very kind', 'We all work together to make sure everyone does well in this class – it doesn't matter which group you are in' and 'She wants to prove to the head teacher that tablets work for spelling!'

Sue's motivation for teaching is that she wants to create a hunger for learning in her class, whereby children always want to improve. She believes that, whatever their starting point, they can always make progress. What makes it all worthwhile for her is seeing one of her most challenging pupils swell with pride, grow and change as he finds ways to make learning work for him and break through his learning barriers.

In this lesson, Sue hardly spoke but the learning and achievement shown by her pupils during these tasks and over time, as shown in their books, demonstrated outstanding progress.

There's no such thing as failure, only feedback.

CHAPTER 6

LEARNING THAT STICKS AND GROWS

One of the most important research discoveries about knowledge and memory in recent years, as reported by Brown et al. in *Make It Stick,* is that active retrieval is the most powerful way to strengthen learning.[1] Making a determined effort to recall information and test yourself works. And the more challenging the test, the more beneficial the impact – so struggling to remember and working very hard at it really does grow your brain. This is especially important for our pupils from disadvantaged families who may not have experienced the drip-feed of continuous answers to their questions as toddlers, or framed explanations or reminders about what goes on in the world around them.

Our recent obsession with tests and exams has led to the conclusion that some teaching in schools is done purely to raise grades, rather than to deliver long-term learning. This is why Ofsted's focus is turning towards teaching to deliver long-term learning, rather than merely cramming for tests with endless practice papers.

Knowledge is power – so is knowing what to do with it!

---

1 Brown et al., *Make It Stick*, p. 59.

We know that learning changes brains. Learning grows new neural pathways and enables us to develop new skills and solve problems. If we want our learners to retain new knowledge long term, they need to secure these pathways by applying new knowledge in novel situations, using it to problem solve and enjoying it! The terminal examinations that now dominate GCSEs require confident mastery and retention of knowledge, not merely rote learning which is shallow and short term. It is essential that we teach our pupils how to review their learning, maximise their memory and grow their neural pathways so that they can perform in examinations and tackle new challenges.

This chapter summarises some of the latest findings from neuroscience and suggests how this can help our pupils retain the essential learning they will need for exams and to develop long-term healthy learning habits.

KNOWLEDGE RETENTION

No matter how well you teach something, it is likely that your pupils will have forgotten most of it within a week, unless they return to it and review it again and again. The challenge for teachers is to make this review process interesting and motivating. We have all heard the moaning protest 'We've done this before, Miss ...' And how often do we reply with 'Yes and we are doing it again and again until you remember it', to a chorus of groans?

Actually, it turns out that although this may not be the best method, it is the best approach.

TYPICAL FORGETTING CURVE FOR NEWLY LEARNED INFORMATION[2]

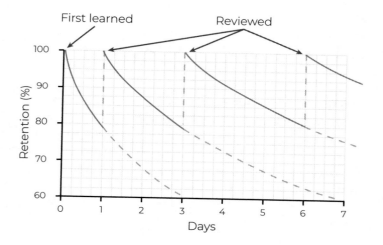

Yes, we forget up to 70% of what we have learned within two days! We need to review information if we want to retain it. The best way to review and revise involves self-testing. So when they say 'We've done it before', your answer should be 'Yes, we have – now let's see what you can remember ...', as you begin a mini test, bingo quiz, cloze exercise or elevator pitch opportunity.

Getting our pupils into the habit of regular self-testing is the most effective way to deepen and master new information. So, we need to teach take-away self-testing techniques. They would prefer that you teach it all again rather than self-test because learning is hard and takes effort. But the harder it is and the more we struggle; the more effective the learning is. Simply rereading information or listening

---

2   Adapted from the work of Hermann Ebbinghaus: H. Ebbinghaus, *Memory: A Contribution to Experimental Psychology*, tr. Henry A. Ruger and Clara E. Bussenius (New York: Teachers College, Columbia University, 1913 [1885]).

again to the same lesson is not as effective as setting ourselves tough tasks to apply the information, or writing or speaking it in our own words.

When learning is harder, it's stronger and lasts longer.[3]

The tried and trusted ways of revising and cramming can give a false sense of security. Pupils may remember more of the stuff, but they won't have a flexible enough grasp on what it means, so when that quirky exam question comes up, they can't take what they know and adapt it wisely. Connecting new knowledge to real-life situations or meta-phorical analogies helps us to deepen our understanding and retain the learning. For example, when you study the principles of heat transfer by conduction, connect to the experience of warming your hands on a cup of hot choco-late. Relate the learning to something – anything – that they already know ...

People who learn to extract the key ideas from new material and organize them into a mental model then connect that model to prior knowledge show an advantage in learning complex mastery.[4]

---

3 Brown, Roediger and McDaniel, *Make It Stick*, p. 9.
4 Brown, Roediger and McDaniel, *Make It Stick*, p. 6.

WE CAN ONLY STORE SO MUCH IN OUR MEMORY BANK

Cognitive load theory (CLT) looks at our 'cognitive architecture' – the way in which we process information – and helps indicate how to teach so that learners will remember more effectively.[5] During learning, information must be held in your working memory until it has been processed sufficiently to pass into your long-term memory. Working memory capacity is very limited, so if too much information is presented at once, it becomes overwhelmed and much of that information is lost. CLT seeks to make learning more efficient by using methods familiar to any good teacher. For example:

- Measuring pupils' present expertise and adapting your teaching accordingly.

- Breaking problems down into parts, and using partially completed problems and worked examples.

- Merging together multiple sources of visual information whenever possible. For example, labelling diagrams.

- Extending the capacity of working memory by using both visual and auditory channels. For example, talking through some information while showing pictures.

Modelling and explaining your own thinking will also help pupils to understand and remember. When a pupil gives a right answer, ask them to verbalise how they thought

---

5   D. Shibli and R. West, Cognitive Load Theory and its Application in the Classroom, *Impact: Journal of the Chartered College of Teaching* (February 2018). Available at: https://impact.chartered.college/article/shibli-cognitive-load-theory-classroom/.

out the answer. Sharing thinking strategies that work is powerful, as they can become contagious.

MAKING CONNECTIONS TO BUILD UNDERSTANDING

Learning always builds on a store of prior knowledge. We remember by building connections to what we already know. Using low-stakes, knowledge-based quizzes in lessons is a great way to review content. Start your lesson by asking five to ten quick questions to test prior learning. This can be done in pairs. Rosenshine suggests conducting a daily review, a weekly review and a monthly review, which connects networks of ideas and means we have to store less in our working memory in order to tackle problems. As working memory is limited, we can only process a small amount of information at once. The more embedded knowledge and understanding we develop over time, the easier it is to deepen and widen this with new related ideas. Tom Sherrington has written a useful book which explains how to apply Rosenshine's common-sense research findings in the classroom.[6] Building in those constant connections with previous learning adds layers of value to your teaching and helps to make sure that the content sticks.

Neural pathways take time and effort to build, and pupils can be reminded that the more often they review and, more importantly, reflect on what they know, the deeper and stronger the pathways become. Metacognition helps pupils to understand how they learn best, by evaluating thinking strategies and reflecting on their progress.

---

6   T. Sherrington, *Rosenshine's Principles in Action* (Woodbridge: John Catt Educational, 2019).

Various timing methods work well to make the review more fun, with pupils seeing how much they can remember in a minute or making up memory stories: 'Once upon a time there was a water molecule ...' Pupils can make up the story from when it fell as a raindrop to evaporating from a leaf or joining a river en route to the sea. Ask your class to create their own games that test their knowledge, working in teams or pairs.

Set homework involving specific tasks that review content, but make them into fun challenges. Pupils could make up the key questions to test their partner with next lesson. They could prepare detailed flashcards for self-testing or knowledge organisers at the end of topics, with the use of colour and imagery to prompt memory. Mind maps work well for some pupils and the act of creating one is a useful process to embed knowledge and see how it connects together.

For some, speaking their learning out loud can help; for others, making posters to put around their bedrooms will embed important ideas. However, it's important for pupils to extend their preferences, as making colourful mind maps *and* audio recordings of their notes will tap into different parts of the brain and embed the learning even more effectively. We need to remember that the harder it is, the more likely it is that the learning will be embedded.

MORE ABOUT METACOGNITION

Since the publication of the Education Endowment Foundation guidance report on metacognition and self-regulated learning we've seen that if pupils can understand how their thinking works when learning, there can be a substantial difference in outcomes.[7] If pupils can monitor their actions and thoughts during task completion and share not only their answers but how they worked them out in their heads, this makes learning more visible. It also encourages pupils to think of better strategies to avoid problems next time and to learn from each other's thinking techniques.

To test your thinking, try to answer this question quickly:

A bat and ball cost £1.10. The bat costs £1 more than the ball. How much does the ball cost?

What was your instinctive answer? (The correct answer is in the footnote.[8]) Was your answer wrong? Now, out loud, talk yourself through the thinking that works out the correct answer. This is the type of verbalising that helps others to understand the thinking steps taken by those who find maths easy.

We often answer with our brain on autopilot, without reflecting on how we got our answer. This is how dual processing can negatively impact learning. Your immediate response feels sort of right, but it can be wrong. When you work out the correct answer, it takes some slow, deductive thinking. The table that follows reflects the difference between unconscious and more studied thinking.[9]

---

7   A. Quigley, D. Muijs and E. Stringer, *Metacognition and Self-Regulated Learning: Guidance Report* (London: Education Endowment Foundation, 2018). Available at: https://educationendowmentfoundation.org.uk/evidence-summaries/teaching-learning-toolkit/meta-cognition-and-self-regulation/.

8   The ball cost 5p. The bat cost £1.05.

9   Adapted from R. H. Thaler and C. R. Sunstein, *Nudge: Improving Decisions About Health, Wealth and Happiness* (London: Penguin, 2009).

Autopilot	Planner
Auto system – gut reaction	Reflective – conscious thought
Fast	Slow
Instinctive	Deductive
Mindless	Self-aware
Unconscious	Conscious
Effortless	Effortful
Reptilian brain	Thinking brain
Default setting	Self-regulating
Status quo bias	Rule following
Homer Simpson!	Dr Spock!

What difference would habitual metacognition have made when you answered the question?

Reflecting on how our thinking works and talking it through as a class or in pairs can really help children to develop the ability to think in new, helpful ways to solve problems. With regular reflection on how our thinking works, we can ensure that successful thinking habits become embedded over time. Strategies for remembering and recalling can be shared and developed.

MNEMONICS

A mnemonic is any learning technique that aids information retention or retrieval (remembering). John Hattie and Gregory Yates reflect on how important parent–child conversations are in developing memory, as parents remind the child of previous events and what they mean.[10] This helps the child understand and learn to respond with their own reflections, in their own words. This type of response makes recall stronger and helps build the capacity for learning and remembering in later life. Schooling takes this ability to a whole new level, but children who have experienced rich conversations at home are clearly at a distinct advantage. It helps them to link new learning with prior knowledge and to develop the strategy of elaboration to help them remember things:

'Look mummy, that car is like nanna's car. It's a red one.'

'Yes Lyla, and it's a Mini – well spotted.'

Such a simple exchange, but relating new observations to prior knowledge is the key to developing the ability to learn and remember. This is elaboration, followed by encoding. Later, a curious question can deepen the knowledge:

'Hey mum, that car is an electric one. Where does it plug in?'

Teachers can play an important role in helping learners to develop these mnemonic skills, especially for children who haven't had the advantage of rich conversations. Good teachers are relentless at weaving in helpful ways to remember stuff when they are teaching children.

---

10 J. Hattie and G. Yates, *Visible Learning and the Science of How We Learn* (Abingdon and New York: Routledge, 2014), p.158.

Techniques such as rhyming, rhythm, stories, acronyms, metaphors, lists, acrostics, rehearsal and repetition are all part of a great teacher's repertoire. (See the examples on pages 162–164.)

Even more important is the teacher's method of questioning, which should develop the pupils' metacognitive abilities. Open questions that help children to reflect on how learning works are very valuable. For example, 'How did you learn that last time?', 'What were you thinking when you worked that one out?', 'How did you manage to learn so much from that mistake?' Regular metacognitive questioning develops habits of recall that can connect and deepen different types of learning, and John Hattie quotes studies that found pupils' scores showed significant improvement after being taught by teachers who routinely focused on memory skills:

> High mnemonic teachers (HMT) were characterised as using high levels of memory-relevant language, such as directly cueing learning good methods and asking students why a particular method might be effective.[11]

TEACHING AS LEARNING

Have you noticed that when you teach something, you also learn it? Researchers led by Aloysius Wei Lun Koh showed that teaching improves the teacher's learning because it compels them to retrieve what they've previously studied.[12] In the same way, this can help your pupils to understand and remember what you have taught

---

11   Hattie and Yates, *Visible Learning and the Science of How We Learn*, p. 163.
12   A. Wei Lun Koh, S. Chi Lee and S. Wee Hun Lim, The Learning Benefits of Teaching: A Retrieval Practice Hypothesis, *Applied Cognitive Psychology* 32(3) (2018): 401–410.

Aim:

To be able to describe the solar system and why the earth has day and night.

1 Find out what the word *orbit* means and in a neat table show how far each planet in our solar system is from the sun.

2 Use the information you found in 1, and a suitable scale, to make a model to show the orbits of the planets.

11 The sun, earth and moon are *approximately spherical bodies.* Note down what this means and be ready to present it to the class.

10 Using a suitable scale, draw the diameters of the sun and the planets.

9 Find a way to use a model of the sun and the rotating earth to explain to the class why we have night and day.

8 What did the scientists named in 7 believe about the solar system?

Work in teams of three or four. Decide who is going to work on each task. You will get credit for neatness and accuracy. Materials and sources of information will be provided.

3 Find out the differences between a *star*, a *planet*, a *dwarf planet* and a *moon*.

4 Find out what a *mnemonic* is. Create one as an easy way of remembering the order of the planets from the sun.

5 Find out the names of ten different moons and show where they are in a table.

6 What is a *geocentric model* and what is a *heliocentric model* of the solar system?

7 Make a table to show when and where these scientists lived: Ptolemy, Alhazen, Galileo and Copernicus.

Group 1. Heart and circulatory system diseases

Tabulate the causes, symptoms and dangers of the following, wherever possible illustrating them with photographs, diagrams, etc.

Aneurysm, angina, arrhythmia, atheroma, cardiovascular disease, excess cholesterol, coronary, hole in the heart, hypertension, myocardial infarction, thrombosis.

You will later present this to the rest of the class.

Group 5. Control of the heartbeat

Prepare an annotated and illustrated flow chart which uses the following terms to describe how the beat is controlled:

Cardiac cycle, autonomic system, vagus nerve, myogenic, septum, atrioventricular node, sinuatrial node, Purkinje fibres, bundle of His, wave of activity.

You will later present this to the rest of the class.

CIRC
S

Group 4. Design and carry out experiments to investigate:

- Resting pulse rate
- Pulse rate during exercise
- Recovery time
- Arterial elasticity

Include cardiac output.

After trialling these, you will lead the rest of the class in carrying out these investigations.

Aim:

For the whole class to be able to interpret pressure and volume data and ECG traces.

Each group must prepare a 40 minute lesson on your topic to teach the rest of the class.

Group 2. The functions of the mammalian circulatory system

Prepare an illustrated talk on the functions of circulatory systems and the advantages of a double circulatory system over a single circulatory system.

Include prepared dissections, drawings and diagrams to show the structure of these parts: arteries, veins, capillaries, arterioles.

You will later present this to the rest of the class.

Group 3. Heart structure

Prepare pinned and labelled heart dissections and diagrams to show the following:

Atria, ventricles, left and right atrioventricular valves, septum, aorta, pulmonary artery and vein, vena cava and coronary artery.

After preparing these, you will lead the rest of the class in carrying out this dissection.

ORY
1

them. An additional advantage is that it builds confidence and communication skills.

Build pupils teaching each other into your schemes of work and lessons as much as possible. Flip the learning and ask them, as homework, to swot up on an aspect of the course, then plan a lesson to teach their partner. On pages 156–159 you will find a couple of examples from Key Stage 2 and Key Stage 5 science, in which pupils take one part of the curriculum and plan to teach it to their peers. Afterwards, you review the learning with the class, fill in any gaps and deepen the learning.[13]

VERBAL REHEARSAL DEEPENS LEARNING

Peer teaching can be time-consuming, so another way is to use the *Dragons' Den* approach and task your class with giving a two-minute pitch recalling their learning on a topic or exam question. They practise it in pairs then volunteers can deliver it to the class. This is hard – you try it and model it yourself first for the class! It's also an opportunity to grow confidence and resilience as well as public speaking skills. Synthesising what you know and speaking it in your own words is a very powerful way to deepen memory, so encourage your class to do this at home. It doesn't matter if they blag it a bit – blagging is improvising. It helps build vocabulary for expressing knowledge in different ways. I should know, I've made a career out of it!

Finally, consider using a Philosophy for Children (P4C) approach to revision to strengthen memory. This involves

---

13 J. Beasley, *The Perfect Science Lesson* (Carmarthen: Independent Thinking Press, 2014).

asking the class, in pairs, to create a philosophical, contro-versial, interesting question about the topic. You'll then have about 15 questions, which you write up on the board. Ask the class to vote for the question they want to debate. When the question is chosen, sit back, keep quiet and allow *them* to discuss and explore it. (First, however, rein-force the rules of good debate – such as speaking one at a time, listening and respecting each other – see Appendix 5 for more on this.) It is better if they are in a circle and you allow *them* to take responsibility for making it a great debate, with as many pupils as possible taking part. During the debate they will be talking, listening, thinking and deepening their understanding. They will be connect-ing the important knowledge with their experience and other learning. I have done this as a revision lesson at A level and found it much more effective than making and reviewing notes. Test them on what they know afterwards to demonstrate how effective discussion and debate can be as a memory technique.

The main thing is to encourage your class to talk, to share their knowledge and to stretch the way they are using and adapting it to strengthen the connections and their neu-ral pathways. This will enable them to respond to the unexpected question in an examination and apply their knowledge with more confidence.

TOP TIPS

If your pupils struggle with recall, teach them memory techniques and help them to reflect on how they think and learn. Tell them how written and spoken self-testing is the best way to build limitless capacity into their own knowledge banks. Encourage pupils to use these techniques:

- Regular self-quizzing. Even when rereading notes, stop every few pages and test yourself.

- Mental rehearsal. Go for a walk and rehearse the information in your head or out loud. Link it to other information to strengthen the connections.

- Pitch. Give a one- or two-minute pitch on a subject. Practise with a friend/partner and get them to feed back to you on what you have missed or misunderstood.

- Teach someone else. Take a topic you struggle with and teach it to someone else. Encourage them to quiz you and ask for repetition.

- Space out/interleave. Space out the learning so that it is learned in chunks. Learn something, then learn something else before coming back to the first thing. This interleaves the learning and helps to make it stick. Cramming a large amount of information for extended periods isn't as effective.

- Problem-solving and hypothesis. Set problems to solve using the knowledge and information you are learning. For example, in geography, apply your knowledge of town planning to assess and solve a problem in your local town.

- Create a hypothesis based on your history knowledge. For example, 'If I lived in the 18th century I would likely die before reaching 40.'

- Ask metacognitive questions when learning. For example, 'How did you work that one out?', 'What learning works best for you?', 'How did you remember that answer?' and 'Does it help to see it in your head when remembering?'

- P4C – take a topic and discuss it among yourselves using a philosophical approach that starts the discussion with a question. (See Appendix 5.)

- Use acrostics such as Never Eat Cakes Eat Salad Sandwiches And Remain Young to remember the spelling of 'necessary'. Acronyms and initialisms also create memorable references. For example, ADHD for attention deficit hyperactivity disorder, SEAL for social and emotional aspects of learning, GIF for graphic interchange format.

- Rhyme, rhythm and music help embed memory, the classic example being the times tables learned through song. (The fact that you can remember jingles such as 'Do the Shake 'n Vac ...' (go on ... you can remember, if you watched TV in 1980!), shows how long-lasting knowledge can be when linked to rhyme, rhythm and music.)

- Pegword schemes such as one is bun, two is shoe, etc.

- Word associations such as 'attend a dance' to remember how to spell attendance or the classic I before E except after C. Subject-specific word associations such as mela, the Italian for apple – how many apples make an entire meal?

- Use metaphors as a powerful way to elicit elaborative thinking. For example, in English, see sentence connectives as little bridges, commas as amber traffic lights, full stops as red ones and exclamation marks as huge potholes in the road.

- Visualisation. In order to remember, we need to stimulate our emotional brain by connecting the information to visual images that surprise or amaze us. Make a shopping list but imagine that the carrots become a marching band, tomatoes splatter on our heads, toilet rolls become a bracelet and coffee is served by a waiter dressed as a rabbit.

- Memory palace. Imagining placing information in memorable locations – like in the home or along the journey to school – can create a 'memory palace' which helps us to recall items by association with the familiar. Creating a narrative stimulates episodic memory, and retelling the story in our heads then brings back the knowledge we need. Imagining that we are placing information on the walls and ceiling of the examination hall can also be a great help when trying to recall vital facts and figures on the day.

Stick it to me – so it stays.

CHAPTER 7

THE POWER OF PEER COACHING

Developing coaching as a tool for staff performance management is a popular choice for schools that are interested in staff well-being and developing a growth mindset culture. However, peer coaching for pupils has proved to be a powerful weapon in the battle against bullying and anxiety – so it shouldn't stop at staff. Research results show a significant positive impact on pupils' mental health and well-being following programmes that develop cross-age coaching and mentoring.[1] Social integration, cooperation between students and communication with families all increased, while incidents involving behaviours like verbal abuse and physical aggression decrease quite dramatically. The results also showed a decrease in self-reported anxiety and depression among pupils, and an increase in self-esteem.

Implementing peer coaching involves training all staff in how coaching works, then training the pupils to coach each other and setting up cross-age pairings so that children have a friend and ally with whom they can share concerns. It has worked best in practice when Year 6 pupils are paired with Year 4s, Year 9s paired with Year 7s and Year 12s paired with Year 9s. The benefits go both ways as

---

1 R. Ferrer-Cascales, N. Albaladejo-Blázquez, M. Sánchez-SanSegundo, I. Portilla-Tamarit, O. Lordan and N. Ruiz-Robledillo, Effectiveness of the TEI Program for Bullying and Cyberbullying Reduction and School Climate Improvement, *International Journal of Environmental Research and Public Health* 16(4), 580 (2016). Available at: https://www.mdpi.com/1660-4601/16/4/580/htm.

children learn how to ask the right questions to support each other and build empathy skills, thereby increasing their own resilience.

The problems of social media addiction, exam pressure, peer group judgement and broken families have all impacted on our young people. Children are the unhappiest they have been for a decade according to the Children's Society's annual report in 2019.[2] The solution could be to create a network of safety and support, not only from teachers but also from other pupils in the school. Having a coaching buddy helps improve well-being and behaviour.

Coaching involves deep listening and simple questions that can stimulate a change in mindset in the coachee, because it holds a mirror up to thinking and allows us to reflect and tweak our minds towards better solutions.

START WITH STAFF COACHING

Training all your staff in the power of coaching so they can see for themselves how it works is the starting point. According to Dr Tim O'Brien, coaching is now seen as a route to staff growth and development and will enhance their potential and performance as well as boosting personal well-being.[3] Coaching holds a supportive mirror up to our thinking and gently challenges our brain so that we develop that useful habit of metacognition.

The hardest thing about being a leader is trying to run a successful team and manage colleagues' performance.

---

2 See M. Weaver, Children in UK Least Happy They Have Been in a Decade, Says Report, *The Guardian* (28 August 2019). Available at: https://www.theguardian.com/society/2019/aug/28/childhood-happiness-lowest-level-in-decade-says-report.

3 As discussed in Morrison McGill, *Mark. Plan. Teach.*, p. 167.

Using a coaching approach to this, rather than a one-size-fits-all one, enhances collaboration and promotes the sharing of strategies that work for individual teachers.

For coaching to work, any coach must first firmly believe that:

- The coachee already has the resources and solutions that they need in order to achieve.

- It is the coach's job to help the coachee discover these.

- People are always doing their best based on what they know.

- Every person is unique.

- People must be seen in terms of their potential, not their past performance.

Qualities of a great coach:

- Sincerity.

- Openness.

- Flexibility.

- Commitment to the coachee's success.

- Self-awareness.

- Good listening skills.

- Excellent communication skills.

- Non-judgemental attitude.

- Empathy.

- Confidentiality and trust.

- Ability to remain consistent and approachable.

- Trust.

- A growth mindset.

With this in mind, coaching can work to deliver high-quality teaching and learning for staff and pupils because coaching:

- Encourages professional dialogue about improving teaching.

- Helps all teachers understand how to improve their classroom practice step by step.

- Is a bespoke approach which helps individuals to find their own ways to improve.

- Is less prescriptive and more productive in getting teachers to implement policy.

- Can change the mindset and morale of teachers.

- Provides a differentiated tool to support performance management.

- Enhances questioning skills which teachers can use in the classroom.

- Improves feedback – teacher-to-teacher and teacher-to-pupil.

- Supports metacognitive processes so that teachers can reflect on progress for themselves and see how it could work for pupils.

- Models how school and classroom leadership works – just as the teachers do, each pupil must take ownership of their own improvement.

More information about how to implement coaching effectively in your school can be found in *The Perfect Teacher Coach*.[4] For coaching to work well, it needs to be embedded as part of the culture of collaboration in the school, without making huge time demands on staff. A simple coaching model, like iSTRIDE (which we'll explore in

---

4   J. Beere and T. Broughton, *The Perfect (Teacher) Coach* (Carmarthen: Independent Thinking Press, 2013).

a moment), might revolve around very focused ten-minute coaching sessions. These promote the implementation of small changes in behaviour – or new solutions to problems – in small steps, with the help of a colleague who listens, asks useful questions and helps evaluate outcomes.

THE iSTRIDE MODEL

There are many models of coaching available but one that is incredibly useful for schools is the iSTRIDE model.[5] What follows is a modified version which is easy to use and implement yet offers a rigorous and flexible approach.

It is only a model. It is not meant to be prescriptive or rigid but organic in nature. Flexibility and adaptability are always essential in allowing the coach to support and meet the coachee's needs. With iSTRIDE, coaches can move backwards and forwards along the continuum that follows, using a blend of techniques appropriate to the coachee (see page 170).

The following questions are tailored to each step of the iSTRIDE model. I hope that you can see how using these types of questions with colleagues and in the classroom will encourage ways of thinking that will help others to own their own change and growth.

---

5   See W. Thomas, *Coaching Solutions Resource Book* (London: Network Continuum Education, 2005), ch. 2.

CONVERSATION

Connection

Questions

Calibration

Reflections

Thinking

Calibration (adjust, adapt, tune in)

Reflections

Thinking

Calibration

Questions

INSIGHT

iSTRIDE COACHING QUESTIONS

Information gathering:

Before the questioning phase, the coach should establish context by learning about the coachee's subject, phase, experience and previous performance.

Strengths:

- What have you tried recently that worked?
- What has made you feel successful this week?
- What has been your best achievement of the year?
- What went well this week?
- Can you tell me about your most sparkling moment as a teacher?
- How does your favourite pupil respond to you?
- What are you most proud of as a teacher?
- When do you perform at your best?

Target/goal:

- What is it that you would like to achieve?
- What would need to happen for you to walk away feeling that this is time well spent?
- What exactly is it that will make you feel successful in this?
- What are you building towards?
- What do you really, really want?
- What don't you want?
- What has to happen for you to feel successful?
- How do you know that this goal is worth achieving?

- How will you know when you have achieved it?
- What will you see, hear and feel after having achieved it?
- What will achieving this goal do for you/give you?
- How would other people benefit if you reached your goal?
- What is important to you about achieving this goal?
- How much personal control do you have over your goal?
- What can you do yourself to achieve this goal?
- By when do you want to achieve it?
- How will you measure it?
- What is your heart telling you about this goal?
- What is your dream outcome?

Reality:

- Where are you starting from/what have you learned so far?
- What have you done so far about this goal?
- How effective have your efforts been?
- What has stopped you doing more?
- What have you learned from what you've done?
- What might you have done differently?
- What insights do you have about yourself/life in general that are relevant to this?
- What will happen if you do nothing?
- What other choices do you have?
- What do you have that you are not using?

- What is holding you back?
- What could stop you achieving your goal?
- What are you afraid of?
- What is not achieving your goal costing you?

Ideas/strategies:

- What could you do?
- What could you do differently from now on?
- What must change for you to achieve your goal?
- What approaches have you seen used in similar circumstances?
- Who might be able to help you?
- Who could you learn from?
- What would a wise old friend suggest?
- What would you do if you had more time/power/money/a magic wand? What about if you had less?
- What is the simplest solution?
- What is the right thing to do?
- What is the most courageous step to take?
- If the constraints were removed, what would you do?
- What else could you do? ... and what else could you do? ... and what else could you do? ...
- What options would you like to act on?
- What could you do that would make the biggest difference?

Decide/commit:

- What is the first logical step?

- What are the next steps?

- Precisely when will you do this?

- What will it cost you if you don't take action?

- What will you gain if you do take action?

- What might get in the way?

- Who needs to know about this?

- What support do you need and from whom?

- How will you get that support?

- Rate on a 1–10 scale (1 being opposed, 10 being totally invested) your motivation to take the agreed actions.

- What prevents you from being at a 10?

- What do you need to do to get your commitment up to at least an 8?

Evaluate:

- What did you do that was different?

- On a scale of 1–10 (1 being not at all, 10 being all-out effort), how hard did you try?

- What was the hardest thing?

- How did it make you feel?

- What has happened since?

- What was the impact (qualitative and quantitative)?

- How have you changed?

- What will you do next?

Once staff are trained, it often works best to ask for volunteers to pilot peer coaching among staff (but this needs to be non-hierarchical). The volunteers can coach each other once a half term and record their targets in a coaching manual. The practice can then be rolled out to all staff and incorporated into staff development programmes so that time and space can be allocated.

INTRODUCING PEER COACHING IN SCHOOL

Once you have trained up staff so that they understand how coaching works and can see the benefits for themselves, coaching can become a powerful force for good throughout the school community. Teachers will already be using more coaching-style questions when dealing with pupils. Leaders will be using micro-coaching as part of their approach to leadership – for example, Brian says to Jeff, 'I really can't get through to my Year 11 this term and it's that crucial time of the year. Can you come and have a word?'

Instead of Jeff leaping in to rescue Brian, Jeff asks coaching questions that encourage reflection on how to resolve the problem. For example:

'What's gone well with your Year 11s this week?'

'How would you like them to be at the moment?'

'What worked well when they've switched off before?'

'Is it all of them?'

'Have *you* been thinking differently recently?'

This habit of promoting reflection by asking coaching questions then listening and responding can also be encouraged in your pupils. Volunteers who coach pupils from other year groups gain valuable listening and coaching experiences. Alternatively, coaching can be set up within year groups or simply be practised within the classroom. Coaching can take place during breaks, after school or in PSHE lessons, but it is useful to set up quiet places where it can take place without interruption. Ten minutes of being truly listened to by a caring peer can enhance resilience and a sense of belonging. It can be particularly valuable at stressful times of the year such as SATs or GCSE exam periods.

CREATING A PEER COACHING PROGRAMME FOR PUPILS: THE SEVEN ESSENTIAL STEPS

1   Train all staff and establish peer coaching partnerships between staff members.

2   Train selected year groups in coaching, so they know about techniques, practice, safeguarding, etc. (See the programme induction example that follows for more ideas about what to include.)

3   Encourage coaching as part of classroom practice.

4   Talk to parents of relevant year groups to outline the plan and gain approval for their child to be included.

5   Take volunteers from selected year groups to become coaches for younger pupils. For example, Year 9 to coach Year 7, Year 12 to coach Year 10, Year 6 to coach Year 5.

6   Appoint a peer coaching leader to oversee the process and build a team of mentors to support the pupil coaches.

7   Organise a meeting for pupil partners. Establish a timeline and guidance for coaching sessions – for example, they are to have monthly meetings and agree the focus for the term and arrangements for oversight.

The coaching group can now meet to feed back on the impact and troubleshoot any problems.

WHAT TO COVER IN A PUPIL PEER COACHING PROGRAMME INDUCTION

This could be delivered to all or just to self-selected pupils.

- A discussion about what coaching is and how it can benefit all of us. (Many will only know coaching as a sporting term so it's important to explain the difference.)
- A discussion about what makes a great coach. (See page 167 for ideas.)
- Answering the questions: 'Why does your mindset matter for success and well-being?' and 'How can coaching help you to have a flexible and resilient mindset?'
- How to conduct an iSTRIDE structured ten-minute coaching session. (See pages 169–175.)
- Practice sessions with a partner and observer, followed by a discussion about how it worked.
- Rules for working with your peers – confidentiality, responsibility, purpose and supervision are essential.
- Arrangements for partnerships.

SELF-COACHING

The added bonus of making coaching central to the school's ethos is that everyone becomes more reflective and self-regulating. The thinking habits outlined in Chapter 1 are key to surviving and thriving in the teaching profession, and they can be enhanced by self-coaching.

In *The Chimp Paradox*, Steve Peters – who has trained the British Olympic cycling team and the snooker player Ronnie O'Sullivan to perform at their best using his mind management programme – talks of 'the Stone of Life', which clarifies your beliefs and values so you can draw on them in moments of crisis.[6] His 'mind management' metaphor suggests that the emotional brain acts like a chimp on our shoulder, which can disempower us with self-doubt and anxiety. He suggests that the secret of health and happiness is to learn to 'manage' the chimp and 'harness its strength and power'.[7]

Growth mindset habits, as outlined in Chapter 1, will help you manage your 'chimp' – and, as a side benefit, you'll also know how to help your pupils manage their chimps (or get them thinking on purpose, to use my terminology)! We all recognise that irrational thinking can sometimes undermine our performance. We can all too easily develop the habits of cynicism, perfectionism or self-flagellation which make us unhappy and stressed.

If you allow unhelpful habits to become your default setting, they will grow undisturbed in your unconscious. Before you know it, you will find yourself:

● Staying late at work.

---

6 S. Peters, *The Chimp Paradox: The Mind Management Programme to Help You Achieve Success, Confidence and Happiness* (London: Penguin, 2013), p. 63.

7 Peters, *The Chimp Paradox*, p. 8.

- Saying yes to that extra duty when you mean no.

- Skipping meetings more often.

- Regularly moaning to like-minded miseries in the staffroom about the kids getting 'dumber' and cheekier.

To avoid this, take time to consciously reflect on your habits and default mindset, and be determined to develop a growth mindset that:

- Values the learning journey.

- Is always open to trying new experiences.

- Pushes you out of your comfort zone.

What I love about teaching is that we are always learning something new about the human condition and about our own vulnerability – the only danger being that we come to think that there is only one way to do anything. The secret to share with our pupils is that there is always another way.[8]

Change is always possible.

---

8 Independent Thinking's mantra! They even wrote a book about it, see: I. Gilbert, *There Is Another Way: The Second Big Book of Independent Thinking* (Carmarthen: Independent Thinking Press, 2015).

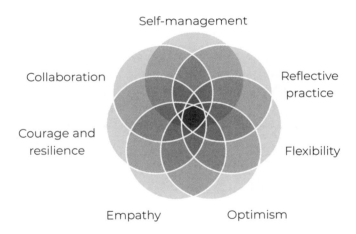

Self-management

Reflective
practice

Flexibility

Optimism

Empathy

Courage and
resilience

Collaboration

CHAPTER 8

WHAT DO I NEED TO DO NEXT TO BE A GREAT TEACHER?

HOW DOES IT ALL WORK IN PRACTICE?

In *The 7 Habits of Highly Effective People*, Stephen Covey offers insights into how to question the drivers of our unconscious mind and start to recognise just how we can think on purpose – instead of by accident.[1] This final chapter recognises how important it is for teachers to do this and brings together Dweck's growth mindset thinking, Hattie's mindframes and the Teachers' Standards[2] to explain and show how to develop the habits you need to be a great teacher.

I've identified seven habits of highly effective teachers.[3] Many of these habits overlap and interact with each other, as we will see.

---

1 S. R. Covey, *The 7 Habits of Highly Effective People* (London: Simon & Schuster, 1989).

2 Department for Education, *Teachers' Standards: Guidance for School Leaders, School Staff and Governing Bodies*. Ref: DFE-00066-2011 (2011). Available at: https://www.gov.uk/government/publications/teachers-standards.

3 See J. Beere, *The Perfect (Ofsted) Inspection* (Carmarthen: Crown House Publishing, 2012), p. 16.

HABIT 1: GREAT SELF-MANAGEMENT

● Be professional in appearance and behaviour – always.

● Always be punctual to lessons and meetings and in completing essential tasks.

● Set ruthless priorities so that everything you do relates to learning and progress for your pupils.

● Develop resilience so you can bounce back after being given critical feedback after a lesson you thought was 'good', or when a normally well-behaved class punish a less inspiring moment with cries of 'This is so boring' or 'I hate geography'.

● Use stress-management strategies – understand how the brain works so that when you panic or feel anxious, you realise that it's normal.

● Take care of your mind and body by eating healthy foods, exercising and keeping up to date with research about education.

● Switch off and relax at home. Put the stresses of the day into a box to be retrieved tomorrow and enjoy time with your partner, children, pets, TV, garden, hobbies ...

Schools can promote a self-management culture through having a powerful and embedded coaching programme, as well as internal and external training events, celebrations of individual achievements, strict attendance, timekeeping and dress policy rules and lots of staffroom cakes, laughs and social events.

To survive and thrive in teaching, you also need to know when to say no and how to prioritise. You can't keep adding more to your to-do list. Ruthlessly prioritise what to innovate and what to abandon to become a better teacher. Here are some examples – but make your own list.

Innovate	Abandon
Use a five-minute lesson plan. (See Appendix 4.)	Writing out long lesson plans.
Try new learning strategies and keep a journal of how well they worked, or didn't.	Marking that doesn't make a difference.
Answer emails immediately and *very* briefly.	Time spent writing detailed email responses.
Use TeachMeets, Twitter and other social media to network for new ideas.	Moaning.
Skim-read books and magazines, jotting down ideas in a learning log.	Listening to moaners.
Take part in everything extracurricular you can manage.	Displacement activity such as texting, checking Facebook or emailing friends.
Get feedback – formal and informal – from pupils and act on it!	Filling in forms.
Phone parents if a child does something good.	Putting up displays (get your artistic pupils to do it!).

HABIT 2: REFLECTIVE PRACTICE

Being a reflective practitioner – using metacognition to stand back and analyse why you respond in certain ways to situations – is contagious. The habit of constantly reviewing how you can improve your teaching, and the learning of your class, also means you'll be more flexible and responsive to your pupils' needs. A trainer can easily spot when teaching staff are habitually reflective. They are curious, self-critical, responsive and take away ideas to play with. They love to be challenged in their thinking and often relish the challenge of change.

Reflective practitioners can reframe a situation and see it another way – and they help pupils do the same. For example, having an inspection is a learning experience and a chance to have your performance appraised and to get useful feedback. As a result, reflective teachers innovate a lot and love coaching each other.

HABIT 3: FLEXIBILITY

Adapting to a changing world, and ever-changing expectations, is an essential habit for pupils and teachers. How flexible are you?

A school culture that values open-minded approaches to teaching and which encourages risk-taking and creativity will encourage flexible approaches to learning. To promote this, such schools have regular cross-curricular events, activity weeks and a range of opportunities for staff to move outside of their comfort zones, including team teaching. This ensures that staff don't get too set in their ways and locked into their subject bunkers.

Flexibility is also developed through personal ownership of change, so regular coaching sessions to help develop outstanding teaching and learning also ensure that teachers are constantly prodded to challenge themselves to find new solutions to problems.

> *If you don't embrace the fact that you think about the world in different ways, you severely limit your chances of finding the person that you were meant to be.*
>
> **KEN ROBINSON**[4]

Robinson recommended several ways to be more flexible and get outside your comfort zone. Try applying them to your working life like this:

- Teach a different subject.

- Try new ways of working – every week.

- Always be on the lookout for new jobs and opportunities.

- Talk to new/different people in the staffroom.

- Use Twitter, Facebook, LinkedIn, etc. to extend your contacts and find new ideas to try in the classroom.

- Visit other schools and lessons regularly – just for fun.

- Team up with other departments or year groups to work together on a learning theme.

- Take part in as many extracurricular activities as you can – especially staff pantos and karaoke.

---

4 K. Robinson, with L. Aronica, *The Element: How Finding Your Passion Changes Everything* (London: Penguin, 2009), p. 49.

- Draw, paint, sing, dance – at whatever level, as often as possible.
- Coach others and yourself to push yourself out of your comfort zone.

HABIT 4: OPTIMISM

There is a four-letter word that is much more important for learning than 'exam' – and that is 'hope'.

Teachers must believe that their pupils can succeed in something. Children must believe that they can improve in anything they set their minds to and be filled with hope and the expectation that they can make progress. Toddlers wake up every morning believing that they can and will learn new things. They show a relentless optimism and determination to learn to walk, talk and find out about the world. We, and our pupils, need to rediscover this and put aside comparisons with others and doubt about ourselves and our abilities.

Optimism about learning and about your own potential to succeed are contagious. So are pessimism and negativity. There is plenty of research evidence to show that optimism can help us succeed,[5] and that creating a culture of optimism and hope in the classroom supports well-being. Some teachers believe that it is important to be realistic rather than optimistic and that it is wrong to raise children's hopes and make them think that they can achieve more than we think they are capable of. But do we know what they are capable of? Have any children gone on to

---

5   See, for example, Martin Seligman's *Flourish: A New Understanding of Happiness and Well-Being – and How to Achieve Them* (London: Nicholas Brealey Publishing, 2011).

achieve amazing things in their adult life even though they were a resounding 'failure' at school? Of course they have!

I once delivered an INSET at a school where everyone seemed to have a deeply held belief that any pupil can achieve an A – no matter how long it takes – if we find the right way to teach them. That school had the best value-added results in the country. Having the habit of optimism also helps develop the resilience (see habit 6) that is essential for learning, so that children can continually reframe failure as an opportunity to learn. Too often we get into the habit of focusing on failure and reliving it over and over again. This is destructive and pointless. When you imagine or remember something, your brain experiences it again, reinforcing those feelings – so why not use this to develop a positive frame of mind? Yes, we have to learn from mistakes, but we can always change what we do to get a different result. Try to:

- Think of your very best moment of teaching this week. Relive it over and over and enhance the good bits to make it even better.

- Reflect on a negative moment and reframe it by saying 'What can I learn from this?'

- Make a list of all the good things about your class, job or team.

- Keep a 'victory log' which tracks all the good things that happen in your class.[6]

- Challenge negative generalisations – such as 'I never get on with Year 8' – with questions – such as 'Which lessons work well with Year 8?'

---

6   For more on victory logs see: A. Vass, The 7 Most Common Mistakes in Classroom Management – and How to Avoid Them! [free factsheet]. Available at: http://www.andyvass.net/pdfs/7commonmistakes0112.pdf.

- Rehearse your dreaded lesson by imagining it going brilliantly as many times as you can.

- Use mantras that focus on success, such as 'If you think you can or if you think you can't, you are right' and 'The harder I work the cleverer I get'.

- Have an optimistic goal that you are working towards. Adapt and adjust it over time.

If you want more ideas and are ready to try something different, read the chapter on challenge in *Teaching Backwards* by Andy Griffith and Mark Burns and implement something new this week.[7]

HABIT 5: EMPATHY

Empathy is part of our natural ability to reflect other people's emotions and thereby understand their perspective on the world. MRI scanning can now detect mirror neurons in our brains that light up when we respond to other people's feelings.[8] This natural tendency to respond to others is the key to altruism and human benevolence. Most teachers go into the profession because they get a kick out of helping others succeed and find nothing more satisfying than turning a challenging class on to learning.

There is another reason why empathy is a most important habit for great teachers: empathetic people are great at getting rapport. As we saw, getting rapport is the aim of that connection and calibration with a class or individual as it elicits wonderful states of cooperation and motivation.

7   Griffith and Burns, *Teaching Backwards*, ch. 5.
8   J. Wood, Brain Imaging Study Reveals the Roots of Empathy, *Psych Central* (8 August 2018). Available at: https://psychcentral.com/news/2017/06/11/brain-imaging-study-reveals-the-roots-of-empathy/121740.html.

Teachers who have high levels of empathy can get kids on side and spread the culture of compassion that is needed to underpin an 'outstanding' school community. They:

- Listen closely to feedback so they can connect and calibrate and adapt their communication.

- Tune in to the pupils in front of them by listening to everything they say and understanding their map of the world.

- Don't take bad behaviour personally but try to understand what is motivating pupils to act out.

- Go to leaders with ideas and solutions – not moans and problems.

HABIT 6: COURAGE AND RESILIENCE

Being creative means breaking the rules – finding new solutions and pushing back the boundaries. This takes courage and confidence as it may go wrong – creativity can be a risky business. That's why it's linked to resilience. You have to be brave, determined and persistent to keep growing as a teacher. We all have our comfort zones, and these mould some of our habitual behaviours – like sitting in the same seat in the staffroom, using the same coffee cup, teaching the same scheme of work and talking to the same colleagues. It feels good to be familiar and comfortable, but great teachers enjoy pushing themselves outside their comfort zones and helping pupils to do the same. You'll know that we all learn best when we are a bit out of our depth and slightly scared. Being ambitious for your classes means having to try new ways of working –

particularly for groups of children who don't learn easily. Courageous, resilient teachers:

- Feed their self-confidence through self-disclosure – are honest about struggling and seek out help.

- Do the things that scare them the most – public speaking, parachuting, taking assembly, running in the teachers' race on sports day …

- Are brave when trying out new strategies – they may not work straight away, so there will be some scary moments.

- Seek out feedback from leaders, pupils and parents because that's how they know how they are doing. They regularly ask their classes 'How am I doing – is this working for you?'

- Have high expectations of themselves but forgive themselves when it goes wrong and learn from it.

- Put themselves in the spotlight.

- Always admit when they are wrong and work out how they will put it right.

- Keep trying with the most challenging pupils or situations. You can't be curious and angry at the same time, so get curious about behaviour!

These teachers have the courage of their convictions and are willing to run workshops on emotionally intelligent parenting to help parents develop these habits for themselves and their children.

HABIT 7: COLLABORATION AND CONNECTION

Human beings were born to collaborate and to learn from one another. The very best teachers love to share ideas and resources and find synergy in the cross-fertilisation of ideas across departments and schools. Whether through informal chats, a Twitter forum or attending conferences and subject workshops, being a good collaborator will enhance your teaching. When teachers develop the habit of collaboration, they pick up the latest thinking, get involved in action research and ensure that their pupils have transferable skills that make essential connections between subjects. Teachers who collaborate well will lead the discourse in school about the vision and values that make it outstanding.

Mentoring, buddying or coaching are essential to embedding collaboration across the school. Training staff about the importance of collaboration – and rewarding and encouraging it – will make a great difference to the feel of the school. Everything from staff karaoke or pantomimes to regular cross-curricular days and mixed-department INSET encourage great collaboration and reconnect us with our mission. We can never underestimate the influence of the 'movers and shakers' on the staff, who are good collaborators and who are always positive and optimistic. They:

- Network in person as often as possible – with different departments, schools, businesses and colleagues in the staffroom and at events.

- Network electronically through Skype and social media, formally and informally.

- Work with different departments on INSET days whenever possible.

- Work closely with and value support staff, governors and business links.

- Mentor new teachers or coach a colleague – learning much about themselves in the process.

- Help with sports days, productions and events for parents.

- Share resources and ideas.

Great collaborators are gold dust. They influence the mood of the school. They aren't always the heads of faculty, but they are the staff members who organise the school social or quiz night and volunteer to lead twilight INSET after they have been on a course.

AND IN THOSE MOMENTS OF WEAKNESS ...

What happens when you wake up at 3 a.m. in August thinking, 'I don't know if I can do this anymore'? We've all done it – no one is a hero at 3 a.m. The most important thing to remember is that, if you track through your career, there have always been – and will always be – moments of crisis, moments of success, periods of excitement and anticipation, and long weeks of exhaustion. You have made and will continue to make mistakes and experience failure. Remember though, the best teachers constantly learn from and support each other and see their job as a lifelong learning experience.

At your best, you are an inspiration, modelling the habits of good learners. At your worst, you are still a learner, acting on feedback – which is no bad thing!

Be the change you want to see.

ATTRIBUTED TO GANDHI

FINAL THOUGHTS

As a trainer of teachers at all stages of their careers, I am constantly in awe of their dedication and passion, and of their determination to make a difference to the young people with whom they work. Beyond the next government initiative, or change in curriculum or exam syllabus, what really matters is what teachers say and do in classrooms to help learners grow into creative, adaptable, industrious and caring people.

Love your job, love the kids and never give up trying to make a difference.

Good luck!

PUPIL LEADERSHIP ROLES

QUIZMASTER Creates a quiz for the class to check learning from last lesson.	**KNOWLEDGE CHECKER** Finds out how much we know by asking key questions during the lesson.
PROGRESS CHECKER Makes sure we are making progress towards our learning outcome(s).	**NUMERACY AMBASSADOR** Looks for any way we can use parts of the lesson to improve our understanding of numbers.
LITERACY AMBASSADOR Looks for any literacy mistakes, and any key words or brilliant vocabulary to celebrate.	**LEAD GREETER** Greets any visitor by explaining what we are doing and how far we have got in the learning.
LEAD CELEBRATOR Celebrates any good things they have seen in the lesson.	**LEAD QUESTIONER** Asks really good questions to help us all understand the lesson a little bit more.
GROWTH MINDSET GURU Makes sure we are all becoming more emotionally intelligent by pushing ourselves out of our comfort zones and showing a positive attitude.	**LEARNING TO LEARN ASSESSOR** Reports on *how* the class has been learning – what is working and what isn't.

RESILIENCE COACH Listens well and asks questions to help others challenge their negative thinking.	**PRINCE/PRINCESS CHARMING** Always polite and helpful. Looks for and celebrates others who are demonstrating these behaviours.
FEEDBACK FANATIC Looks and listens for great written or verbal feedback which helps people learn.	**COMMUNICATIONS COACH** Helps people to speak up in class about what and how they are learning.
CRITICAL FRIEND Gives great written or verbal feedback which helps other people learn.	**CURIOSITY CATCHER** Celebrates people who ask lots of questions about what we are doing and how to do it.
CRITERIA CHECKER Makes sure that everyone knows and understands what makes our work great.	**WAGOLL WIZARD** Checks that people know what a good one looks like.

APPENDIX 2

GROWTH MINDSET HEALTH CHECK

Give yourself a score from 1 to 4 to indicate how often you agree with these statements and demonstrate these behaviours.

1 = Always. 2 = Often. 3= Sometimes. 4 = Rarely.

Do you ...	Score
Believe intelligence is learnable?	
Always see mistakes as learning opportunities?	
Enjoy new challenges and feel comfortable with change?	
Know how you learn best?	
Enjoy a challenge in which you have to make maximum effort?	
Ask for help when you need it?	
Try out new things every day?	
Feel comfortable meeting new people?	
Have a list of new hobbies you would like to try?	
Know how to motivate yourself to work hard when you need to?	
Go to places on your own?	

Do you ...	Score
Renew your goals regularly?	
Find change easy to manage?	
Get inspired when other people enjoy success and learn from them?	
Find it easy to manage difficult conversations?	
Enjoy a good philosophical or political discussion with a range of views?	
Change your mind and views sometimes?	
Get asked for your advice and guidance by friends and family?	
Like to try new activities, places, films and food as often as possible?	
Consider yourself to be a learner above everything else?	
Give honest feedback in order to make progress in a project?	
Ask for feedback from colleagues and pupils?	
Stay up to date with social media, technology, etc.?	
Have ways to quieten your mind when necessary?	
Listen to others and try to understand the way they see the world?	

Consider how you can improve any scores of 3 or 4 as your priority targets.

Targets:

EXTEND YOUR LEARNING MINDSET

This is a resource that you can give to the pupils to encourage them to think about how they are engaging in learning at home.

PUPIL SHEET

We want to give you credit for all the learning you do at home. Earn points for doing the things that push you out of your comfort zone.

Ideas for your extended learning at home:

Around the house	Hobbies/sports	Technology	Other
Cooking/cleaning	Teams	Computer games	Charity work
Gardening	Crafts/art	Internet research	Holidays
Fixing things	Guides/Scouts	Filming	Boot sales/garage sales
Hosting friends	Army cadets	Photography	
Helping neighbours	Keep fit/gym	Tablet/laptop – downloading etc.	
Washing/ironing	Swimming	Communication networks	
Decorating	Drama/dance	Mobile phone	
Looking after pets	Chess/games	Films	
Car washing and maintenance	Music/singing/karaoke		
	Walking/cycling		
	Reading books/magazines		

LEARNING DIARY

Learning diary example

Activity	Commentary	Growth mindset learning points	Points
Cooked an omelette	Never cooked before, so got advice. Mix up eggs and milk, added salt and pepper. Melted butter in pan but it got a bit stuck.	Courage Seeking advice Deferred gratification Making mistakes – as dropped shell in mixture first time	5 points
Army cadets	Went as usual and learned to march in time.	Teamwork Self-management Purposeful practice	3 points
Facebook/ Instagram/ Snapchat	Found out how to upload/download pictures. Create a podcast/vlog to publish. Reviewed internet safety rules.	Communication Creativity Research Learning from mistakes	3 points

Learning diary example			
Activity	Commentary	Growth mindset learning points	Points
Pets	Fed neighbour's cat as they are on holiday. It doesn't like water near its food! Gave it TLC too.	Taking responsibility Empathy Challenge – as I don't like cats	5 points

Points are scored for the effort shown and variety of out-of-school activity. The idea is to do lots of different things at home and discuss how they help you learn. Your record sheet will be discussed with your teacher/tutor/peer coach.

TARGET

Try to do as many different activities as you can at home this term and note what they are in this table. Assign the points you think you should earn from these activities. More points for more challenge! *You* decide …

A FIVE-MINUTE LESSON PLAN

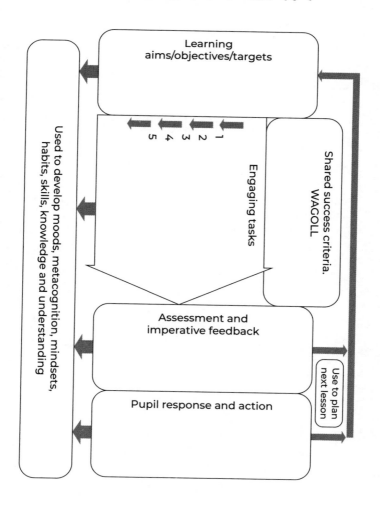

PHILOSOPHY FOR CHILDREN (P4C)

P4C is a 'thinking skills' intervention introduced by SAPERE (Society for Advancing Philosophical Enquiry and Reflection in Education) based on the work of Matthew Lipman. Interventions show improvements in pupils' reasoning and comprehension skills, and, additionally, in their social and emotional development. At its centre is the focus on a 'community of enquiry', in which a group of people, through dialogue, become more open to the views of others, growing through respect for others and developing their own way of thinking – their own philosophy.

This is an adapted plan which you can try in the classroom.

STRUCTURE OF A COMMUNITY OF ENQUIRY

PREPARATION

Sit in a circle so that everyone can make eye contact.

Establish agreed conduct:

● Listen to the speaker.

● Respond to the dialogue (thinking about what is being said).

- Give reasons (I agree/disagree with X because …).

- Treat everyone's contribution with respect.

- Comment on the point, not the person.

- Contribute to support the community.

STIMULUS

This could be a story, video clip, picture, poem, piece of music or key facts. This is to stimulate the discussion, so it should be relevant and engaging.

THINKING TIME

The pupils may need additional resources: sticky notes to write on and move around to focus thinking, a key word record or feelings record.

GENERATE QUESTIONS

In pairs, think of a question that could be used as a possible enquiry.

A brief explanation of the question is given by each questioner, followed by reflection and queries raised by the group.

Each question is written up for everyone to see.

VOTING FOR THE FAVOURITE QUESTION

Use some form of voting to identify the enquiry question – give each student two votes.

FIRST WORDS

The creator of the chosen question opens the discussion by sharing their ideas.

BUILDING

Arrange for pupils to sit in a circle and remind them of the rules of respectful listening. The discussion now opens to everyone, although the teacher should act as facilitator and should not give opinions. It's important that everyone can give their contribution to the dialogue.

FINAL WORDS (AFTER 20–30 MINUTES OF DISCUSSION)

- Students could write their response to the question now, followed by reflection of whether and, if so, how their personal views have changed.

- Each person in turn is given the opportunity to say what they think (there should be no interruption to their exposition) with the pupil who posed the question being the last to speak.

- Following personal reflection, give the students a chance to reflect on the process – who has been a good listener, who has empathised the most, who has showed courage in sharing something personal, etc.?

REFERENCES AND FURTHER READING

Alfieri, L., Brooks, P. J., Aldrich, N. J. and Tenenbaum, H. R. (2011) Does Discovery-Based Instruction Enhance Learning?, *Journal of Educational Psychology* 103(1): 1–18.

Beasley, J. (2014) *The Perfect Science Lesson* (Carmarthen: Independent Thinking Press).

Beere, J. (2012) *The Perfect (Ofsted) Inspection* (Carmarthen: Crown House Publishing).

Beere, J. (2016) *Grow: Change Your Mindset, Change Your Life – a Practical Guide to Thinking on Purpose* (Carmarthen: Crown House Publishing).

Beere, J. (2016) *The Perfect Lesson*, rev edn (Carmarthen: Independent Thinking Press).

Beere, J. and Broughton, T. (2013) *The Perfect (Teacher) Coach* (Carmarthen: Independent Thinking Press).

Berger, R. (2003) *An Ethic of Excellence: Building a Culture of Craftsmanship with Students* (Portsmouth, NH: Heinemann).

Broadfoot, P., Daugherty, R., Gardner, J., Harlen, W., James, M. and Stobart, G. (2002) Assessment for Learning: 10 Principles. Research-Based Principles to Guide Classroom Practice (Assessment Reform Group). Available at: https://www.researchgate/net/publication/271849158_Assessment_for_Learning_10_Principles_Research-based_principles_to_guide_classroom_practice_Assessment_for_Learning.

Broadwell, M. M. (1969) Teaching for Learning (XVI), *The Gospel Guardian* (20 February). Available at: http://www.wordsfitlyspoken.org/gospel_guardian/v20/v20n41p1-3a.html.

Brown, P. C., Roediger, H. L. and McDaniel, M. A. (2014) *Make It Stick: The Science of Successful Learning* (Cambridge, MA: The Belknap Press).

Covey, S. R. (1989) *The 7 Habits of Highly Effective People* (London: Simon & Schuster).

Covey, S. R. (1998) *The 7 Habits of Highly Effective Families* (London: Simon & Schuster).

Curran, A. (2008) *The Little Book of Big Stuff About the Brain* (Carmarthen: Crown House Publishing).

Department for Education (2011) *Teachers' Standards: Guidance for School Leaders, School Staff and Governing Bodies*. Ref: DFE-00066-2011. Available at: https://www.gov.uk/government/publications/teachers-standards.

Duhigg, C. (2012) *The Power of Habit: Why We Do What We Do and How to Change* (London: William Heinemann).

Dweck, C. (2006) *Mindset: The New Psychology of Success* (New York: Ballantine Books).

Dweck, C. (2014) The Power of Yet [video], *TEDxNorrköping* (12 September). Available at: https://www.youtube.com/watch?v=J-swZaKN2Ic.

Ebbinghaus, H. (1913 [1885]) *Memory: A Contribution to Experimental Psychology*, tr. H. A. Ruger and C. E. Bussenius (New York: Teachers College, Columbia University).

Elder, Z. (2012) *Full On Learning: Involve Me and I'll Understand* (Carmarthen: Crown House Publishing).

Engelmann, S. (1992) *War Against the Schools' Academic Child Abuse* (Portland, OR: Halcyon House).

Fairclough, M. (2016) *Playing with Fire: Embracing Risk and Danger in Schools* (Woodbridge: John Catt Educational).

Ferrer-Cascales, R., Albaladejo-Blázquez, N., Sánchez-SanSegundo, M., Portilla-Tamarit, I., Lordan, O. and Ruiz-Robledillo, N. (2016) Effectiveness of the TEI Program for Bullying and Cyberbullying Reduction and School Climate Improvement, *International Journal of Environmental Research and Public Health* 16(4), 580. Available at: https://www.mdpi.com/1660-4601/16/4/580/htm.

Frankl, V. (1984 [1959]) *Man's Search for Meaning* (New York: Pocket Books).

Gadsby, C. (2012) *Perfect Assessment for Learning* (Carmarthen: Independent Thinking Press).

Gawdat, M. (2017) *Solve for Happy: Engineer Your Path to Joy* (London: Bluebird).

Gilbert, I. (2007) *The Little Book of Thunks: 260 Questions to Make Your Brain Go Ouch!* (Carmarthen: Independent Thinking Press).

Gilbert, I. (2010) *Why Do I Need a Teacher When I've Got Google?* (Abingdon and New York: Routledge).

Gilbert, I. (2015) *There Is Another Way: The Second Big Book of Independent Thinking* (Carmarthen: Independent Thinking Press).

Gilbert, I. (2017) *The Compleat Thunks Book* (Carmarthen: Independent Thinking Press).

Gladwell, M. (2008) *Outliers: The Story of Success* (London: Penguin).

Goleman, D. (1996) *Emotional Intelligence: Why It Matters More Than IQ* (London: Bloomsbury).

Gregory, S. (2012) National Director Education and Early Years Introduces the Schools Report 2011/12 [video] (27 November). Available at: https://webarchive.nationalarchives.gov.uk/video/Ofstednews/dFhCvzoBYM8.

Griffith, A. and Burns, M. (2014) *Teaching Backwards* (Carmarthen: Crown House Publishing).

Hargreaves, D. (chair) (2005) *About Learning: Report of the Learning Working Group* (London: Demos).

Hattie, J. (2012) *Visible Learning for Teachers: Maximizing Impact on Learning* (Abingdon and New York: Routledge).

Hattie, J. and Yates, G. (2014) *Visible Learning and the Science of How We Learn* (Abingdon and New York: Routledge).

Higgins, S. (2015) A Recent History on Teaching Thinking. In R. Wegerif, L. Li and J. Kaufman (eds), *The Routledge International Handbook of Research on Teaching Thinking* (Abingdon and New York: Routledge), pp. 19–28.

Higgins, S., Kokotsaki, D. and Coe, R. J. (2011) *Toolkit of Strategies to Improve Learning: Summary for Schools Spending the Pupil Premium* (London: Sutton Trust).

Hook, P. and Vass A. (2000) *Confident Classroom Leadership* (London: David Fulton).

Jackson, N. (2009) *The Little Book of Music for the Classroom: Using Music to Improve Memory, Motivation, Learning and Creativity* (Carmarthen: Independent Thinking Press).

Jones, W. (2017) A Third of Kids Are Written Off as Failures. It Doesn't Have to Be This Way, *National Numeracy* [blog] (14 March). Available at: https://www.nationalnumeracy.org.uk/blog/third-kids-are-written-failures-it-doesnt-have-be-way.

Kahneman, D. (2012) *Thinking, Fast and Slow* (London: Penguin).

Kirby, J. (2015) Knowledge Organisers, *Pragmatic Reform* [blog] (28 March). Available at: https://pragmaticreform.wordpress.com/2015/03/28/knowledge-organisers/.

Lang, J. M. (2013) *Cheating Lessons: Learning from Academic Dishonesty* (Cambridge, MA: Harvard University Press).

Lee, J. (2013) Open Your Mind to the Teachings of Neuroscience, *Times Educational Supplement* (1 March). Available at: https://www.tes.com/news/open-your-mind-teachings-neuroscience.

Lemov, D. (2015) *Teach Like a Champion 2.0: 62 Techniques That Put Students on the Path to College* (San Francisco, CA: Jossey-Bass).

Morrison McGill, R. (2017) *Mark. Plan. Teach.* (London: Bloomsbury Education).

Ofsted (2019) Education Inspection Framework 2019: Inspecting the Substance of Education [consultation outcome] (29 July). Available at: https://www.gov.uk/government/consultations/education-inspection-framework-2019-inspecting-the-substance-of-education/education-inspection-framework-2019-inspecting-the-substance-of-education.

Ofsted (2019) *School Inspection Handbook*. Ref: 190017. Available at: https://www.gov.uk/government/publications/school-inspection-handbook-eif.

Peters, S. (2013) *The Chimp Paradox: The Mind Management Programme to Help You Achieve Success, Confidence and Happiness* (London: Penguin).

Quigley, A., Muijs, D. and Stringer, E. (2018) *Metacognition and Self-Regulated Learning: Guidance Report* (London: Education

Endowment Foundation). Available at: https://educationendowmentfoundation.org.uk/evidence-summaries/teaching-learning-toolkit/meta-cognition-and-self-regulation/.

Robinson, K. with Aronica, L. (2009) *The Element: How Finding Your Passion Changes Everything* (London: Penguin).

Rosenshine, B. (2012) Principles of Instruction: Research-Based Strategies That All Teachers Should Know, *American Educator* 36(1): 12–19, 39.

Rosenshine, B., Meister, C. and Chapman, S. (1996) Teaching Students to Generate Questions: A Review of Intervention Studies, *Review of Educational Research* 66: 181–221.

Rowling, J. K. (2008) The Fringe Benefits of Failure, and the Importance of Imagination. Speech delivered at the Harvard University Commencement (5 June). Transcript available at: https://news.harvard.edu/gazette/story/2008/06/text-of-j-k-rowling-speech/.

Salles, D. (2016) *The Slightly Awesome Teacher: Edu-Research Meets Common Sense* (Woodbridge: John Catt Educational).

Seligman, M. (2011) *Flourish: A New Understanding of Happiness and Well-Being – and How to Achieve Them* (London: Nicholas Brealey Publishing).

Sherrington, T. (2019) *Rosenshine's Principles in Action* (Woodbridge: John Catt Educational).

Shibli, D. and West, R. (2018) Cognitive Load Theory and Its Application in the Classroom, *Impact: Journal of the Chartered College of Teaching* (February). Available at: https://impact.chartered.college/article/shibli-cognitive-load-theory-classroom/.

Sweller, J. (1998) Cognitive Load During Problem Solving: Effects on Learning, *Cognitive Science* (12): 257–285.

Thaler, R. H. and Sunstein, C. R. (2009) *Nudge: Improving Decisions About Health, Wealth and Happiness* (London: Penguin).

Thomas, W. (2005) *Coaching Solutions Resource Book* (London: Network Continuum Education).

Tuckman, B. (1965) Developmental Sequence in Small Groups, *Psychological Bulletin* 63(6): 384–399.

Vass, A. (n.d.) The 7 Most Common Mistakes in Classroom Management – and How to Avoid Them! [free factsheet]. Available at: http://www.andyvass.net/pdfs/7commonmistakes0112.pdf.

Wall, K., Hall, E., Baumfield, V., et al. (2010) *Learning to Learn in School Phase 4 and Learning to Learn in Further Education* (London: Campaign for Learning).

Waters, M. (2013) *Thinking Allowed on Schooling* (Carmarthen: Independent Thinking Press).

Watson, P. (2013) Most Teachers Reach a Performance Plateau Within a Few Years According to Research, *Montrose 42* [blog] (12 April). Available at: https://montrose42.wordpress.com/2013/04/12/most-teachers-reach-a-performance-plateau-within-a-few-years-according-to-research/.

Weaver, M. (2019) Children in UK Least Happy They Have Been in a Decade, Says Report, *The Guardian* (28 August). Available at: https://www.theguardian.com/society/2019/aug/28/childhood-happiness-lowest-level-in-decade-says-report.

Wei Lun Koh, A., Chi Lee, S. and Wee Hun Lim, S. (2018) The Learning Benefits of Teaching: A Retrieval Practice Hypothesis, *Applied Cognitive Psychology* 32(3): 401–410.

West-Burnham, J. and Coates, M. (2006) *Transforming Education for Every Child: A Practical Handbook* (London: Network Educational Press).

Wiliam, D. and Black, P. (2006) *Inside the Black Box: Raising Standards Through Classroom Assessment* (London: GL Assessment).

Willingham, D. T. (2009) *Why Don't Students Like School? A Cognitive Scientist Answers Questions About How the Mind Works and What It Means for the Classroom* (San Francisco, CA: Jossey-Bass).

Wood, J. (2018) Brain Imaging Study Reveals the Roots of Empathy, *Psych Central* (8 August). Available at: https://psychcentral.com/news/2017/06/11/brain-imaging-study-reveals-the-roots-of-empathy/121740.html.

978-178135337-0

978-178135338-7

978-178135339-4

978-178135340-0

978-178135341-7

978-178135353-0

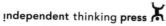

www.independentthinkingpress.com

978-178135317-2

978-178583011-2

978-178135003-4

ındependent thinking **press**

www.independentthinkingpress.com

There
is
Another Way

The Second Big Book of
Independent Thinking

Ian Gilbert

978-178135236-6

independent thinking

Independent Thinking. An education company.

Taking people's brains for a walk since 1994.

We use our words.

www.independentthinking.com